JONI HYDE

The Order of Grace

How God Chooses - and Why His Mercy Comes First

Joni Hyde,
INC

Contents

Preface

This book did not begin at a desk. It began in a church pew, with a Bible open, listening to the steady, faithful preaching of God's Word.

The material you are about to read was shaped during a season of sitting under a series of sermons on Romans 9–11 taught by my pastor, Tim Senn, in Little Rock, Arkansas. Week after week, I listened as Paul's words were opened carefully and patiently, words that are not casual or shallow, but deliberate, weighty, and precise.

During that same season, not because of those sermons, but alongside them, the Lord placed a quiet prayer on my heart. As a grandmother, thinking about my grandchildren and the generations still to come, I found myself asking a simple but searching question:

What can I pass on that will be of lasting substance to their faith? What truly matters, and what will endure?

That prayer first took shape as a desire to write a children's book. I wanted to explain saving grace in a way young hearts could grasp, by using simple language, gentle images, and truths small enough to hold. I imagined something tender and clear, something that could help frame their understanding of God early and well.

With that hope in mind, I began transcribing, studying, praying over, and working carefully through the sermons line by line. What began as preparation for a children's book quickly revealed something else. As I worked, it became clear that I needed to slow down.

Paul's words in Romans demanded more careful attention. Before these truths could be simplified responsibly for children, they had to be understood more deeply. I needed to trace Paul's arguments, feel their tension, and see how God's sovereignty, human responsibility, grace, mercy, warning, and hope fit together without distortion.

In that slowing down, I began to see the Lord's redirection.

Before the children's book could be written, this book needed to exist. I needed space to work through what Paul is saying, not as an academic exercise, but as a foundation, so that these truths could be understood clearly and passed on with care.

In this process, I was careful not to receive the sermons I was studying simply because they were preached clearly or spoken persuasively. Every claim, every conclusion, and every theological thread was tested against Scripture itself. Again and again, I returned to the text, asking one steady question: "Is this actually what God has said?" My aim was to let the Word of God speak with its own weight and clarity, trusting that Scripture itself is sufficient, coherent, and trustworthy. Having walked slowly through these truths, I now see more clearly how faith-shaping they are. They steady the heart. They humble pride. They remove fear. And they teach us to trust God, not only with our own salvation, but with the salvation of those we love most.

This deeper understanding has brought me back to the prayer that first stirred this work. Holding my grandchildren, Lauren and Drew, and thinking about the generations still to come, I find myself returning to the same request and still asking, still learning, but even more aware of how much depends on the Lord's kindness rather than my clarity.

As a grandparent, I know I cannot control belief or manufacture faith. But I can seek to teach what is true with care and humility. I can speak of a God who saves by grace. And I can help, however imperfectly, to frame their understanding of Him as sovereign, kind, patient, and trustworthy, and to support their parents as they do the same.

That is how this book came to be. While Romans 9 forms the heart of this study, Paul's argument does not stop there. As I worked slowly through these chapters, it became clear that Romans 10 and 11 are not side notes or afterthoughts, but necessary companions. Together, they show not only God's sovereign mercy in choosing, but how that mercy is received by faith, proclaimed through the gospel, and revealed as faithful, patient, and good. For that reason, this book lingers longest in Romans 9, but follows Paul carefully into Romans 10 and 11, allowing the full shape of his argument to unfold as he intended.

This book sits alongside the life of the local church, not above it. I am not a pastor or a theologian by training. I am a learner in the church, a Mom, and now a Mimi, continuing to be shaped and sanctified by the faithful ministry of God's Word. These pages reflect the posture of someone sitting under Scripture and wanting to help others do the same.

I am deeply grateful for a pastor who labors week after week to open the Scriptures with clarity and courage, and for a church that values truth spoken patiently and carefully. Any insight found here is a reflection of that gift. Any clarity belongs to the Word itself. And any mistakes are mine alone.

My hope is that this book feels less like a lecture and more like a walk through difficult but necessary truths that steadies rather than overwhelms. And for young adults, parents, grandparents, teachers, and all who influence young hearts, a walk that replaces fear with trust and control with confidence in the kindness of God.

This book is dedicated to my daughter Lindsey and son-in-law Glenn, with the hope that God's Word will continue to shape our family across generations. It is written with prayer and trust that long after my efforts are complete, Scripture will remain, doing what only God can do.

If these pages do what I hope they do, they will not be an ending, but a beginning. The truths explored here are not meant to stay confined to careful study or adult understanding alone, but to be carried forward, spoken simply, lived faithfully, and shared with love. This book lays a foundation. Whatever grows from it, I trust the Lord to shape in His time.

With gratitude,
Joni Hyde

Acknowledgments

I am deeply grateful to the Lord for His steady kindness and for the faithful ways He has shaped my life through His Word. I give special thanks to Pastor Tim Senn, who has opened Scripture carefully and patiently over many weeks, and to a church family committed to truth spoken with clarity and grace,

I am thankful for my daughter, Lindsey, and my son-in-law, Glenn, whose daily faithfulness as parents continues to remind me that the most important work of faith often happens slowly, in ordinary moments, over time. I am also grateful for friends who walked alongside me during this season with prayers and quiet support.

Any clarity found in these pages is a gift from the Lord; any remaining weakness belongs to me alone. My hope is simply that this book might play a small role in a longer walk of faith— one that continues beyond these pages and, in time, into the lives of others.

1

Chapter 1

God's Faithfulness Under Question

This book studies Romans 9–11 as a unified section of Paul's letter, with particular attention given to Romans 9, where the central questions are first raised. What Paul introduces in chapter 9, continues into chapters 10 and 11, where those themes are developed and brought to resolution.

The first chapter of this book will begin with a broad overview of Romans 9 itself. This flyover is meant to orient us, to show the shape and movement of Paul's argument, before we slow down and walk carefully through the text in detail.

However, before moving forward to our starting point in Romans 9, it is important to step back to the close of Romans 8, where Paul declares one of the strongest assurances in all of Scripture. He has just finished proclaiming the security of those who are in Christ, an assurance that nothing in creation can separate the believer from the love of God.

Romans 8:38–39
38 For I am convinced that neither death, nor life, nor angels, nor rulers, nor things present, nor things to come, nor powers, 39 nor height, nor depth, nor any other created thing will be able to separate us from the love of God, which is in Christ Jesus our Lord.

This is not a minor or passing statement. It is the summit of Paul's message so far. Paul ends Romans 8 with great confidence, certainty, and hope that cannot be shaken by suffering, failure, or opposition.

But it is precisely because this assurance is so strong that what follows matters so deeply.

Paul realizes he must address something that appears to strain everything he has just said. If God's love is truly unbreakable, if His purposes truly stand, then how are we to understand the widespread unbelief of Israel, the people to whom God first gave His promises? Has God's word failed? Have His purposes shifted? Or is there something deeper unfolding that must be understood if this assurance is to remain trustworthy?

Romans 9–11 exists because Romans 8 is true. Paul does not present these chapters as a theological aside, nor as a new topic disconnected from what came before. He turns to them because the confidence he has just declared demands an explanation that can withstand hard questions. Only by addressing them can Paul show that the security promised to believers rests on a God whose faithfulness does not fracture under pressure. It is here that Paul begins a sustained and careful explanation across Romans 9, 10, and 11, meant to show why that assurance can be trusted, even when God's ways are difficult to trace.

What follows requires us to slow down, listen closely, and learn to trust that God's mercy is both deeper and more faithful than it may first appear. Before we settle into the details, we continue here with a brief flyover of Romans 9 to see the shape of Paul's argument.

God's Irrevocable Promises

Romans 9:1–3

Paul opens this section with anguish, not abstraction. His sorrow over Israel's unbelief is unmistakable. Though he has just proclaimed the unshakable security of those who are in Christ, that confidence has not dulled his compassion. It has deepened it.

1 I am telling the truth in Christ, I am not lying, my conscience testifies with me in the Holy Spirit,
2 that I have great sorrow and unceasing grief in my heart.
3 For I could wish that I myself were accursed, separated from Christ for the sake of my brothers, my kinsmen according to the flesh,

Paul's words are startling. He speaks of "great sorrow" and "unceasing grief." His love for Israel is not theoretical. He aches for them. He longs for their salvation, even to the point of expressing a willingness to bear loss himself if it could bring them life.

This sorrow frames everything that follows. Romans 9 is not

written from a distance. It rises out of love, grief, and a longing to see God's promises fulfilled.

Israel's Incredible Privileges

Romans 9:4–5

Paul reminds his readers that Israel was not overlooked or neglected by God. They were entrusted with extraordinary privileges.

4 who are Israelites, to whom belongs the adoption as sons, and the glory and the covenants and the giving of the Law and the temple service and the promises,

5 whose are the fathers, and from whom is the Christ according to the flesh, who is God over all, blessed forever. Amen.

Israel's blessings included adoption as sons, God's manifest presence, the covenants, the Law, the worship of the temple, the promises, the patriarchs, and even the Messiah Himself. These privileges magnify the tragedy of Israel's unbelief, but they also set the stage for Paul's central concern.

If Israel possessed all of this and yet remains largely unbelieving, has God's word failed?

The First Objection Is Anticipated

Romans 9:6–9

Paul addresses the anticipated question before it is even spoken.

6 But it is not as though the word of God has failed. For they are not all Israel who are descended from Israel;
7 nor are they all children because they are Abraham's seed, but: "Through Isaac your seed will be named."
8 That is, the children of the flesh are not the children of God, but the children of the promise are considered as seed.
9 For this is the word of promise: "At this time I will come, and Sarah shall have a son."

From the beginning, God has distinguished between physical descent and spiritual promise. Belonging to Israel has never been merely a matter of birth. It has always been rooted in God's promise and purpose.

God's Sovereign Election

Romans 9:10–13

Paul presses deeper by pointing to Jacob and Esau.

10 And not only this, but there was Rebekah also, when she had conceived twins by one man, our father Isaac;

11 for though the twins were not yet born and had not done anything good or bad, so that the purpose of God according to His choice would stand, not because of works but because of Him who calls,

12 it was said to her, "The older shall serve the younger."

13 Just as it is written, "Jacob I loved, but Esau I hated."

God's choice was made before action, effort, or merit entered the picture. Election, as Paul presents it here, simply names God's purposeful choosing, His decision to act in mercy according to His own call rather than human qualification. It magnifies grace, removes boasting, and anchors salvation in God's mercy alone.

Paul Anticipates the Next Objection

Romans 9:14–16

Is God unjust?

14 What shall we say then? Is there any unrighteousness with God? May it never be!

15 For He says to Moses, "I will have mercy on whom I have mercy, and I will have compassion on whom I have compassion."

16 So then it does not depend on the one who wills or the one who runs, but on God who has mercy.

Paul does not soften the truth. God's mercy is free, deliberate, and undeserved. Justice is not compromised by mercy; mercy reveals God's glory.

God's Purpose Displayed

Romans 9:17–18

Paul turns to Pharaoh.

17 For the Scripture says to Pharaoh, "For this very purpose I raised you up, in order to demonstrate My power in you, and in order that My name might be proclaimed throughout the whole earth."
18 So then He has mercy on whom He desires, and He hardens whom He desires.

God is not reacting. He is revealing Himself. His purposes stand, even when human hearts resist Him.

The Creator and the Clay

Romans 9:19–21

Another objection follows.

19 You will say to me then, "Why does He still find fault? For who resists His will?"
20 On the contrary, who are you, O man, who answers back to God? Will the thing molded say to the molder, "Why did you make me like this"?
21 Or does not the potter have authority over the clay, to make

from the same lump one vessel for honorable use and another for dishonorable use?

Paul reorients us. God is the potter. We are the clay. This is not cruelty. It is creator to creature reality.

Vessels of Wrath and Mercy

Romans 9:22–23

22 And what if God, wanting to demonstrate His wrath and to make His power known, endured with much patience vessels of wrath having been prepared for destruction,
23 and in order that He might make known the riches of His glory upon vessels of mercy, which He prepared beforehand for glory.

God's patience is real. His mercy is intentional. Salvation is not accidental.

The Inclusion of the Gentiles and the Preservation of Israel

Romans 9:24–29

24 even us, whom He also called, not from among Jews only, but also from among Gentiles?
25 As He says also in Hosea, "I will call those who were not My people, 'My people,' And her who was not beloved, 'beloved.'"
26 "And it shall be that in the place where it was said to them, 'you are not My people, There they shall be called sons of the living God."
27 And Isaiah cries out concerning Israel, "Though the number of the sons of Israel be like the sand of the sea, it is the remnant that will be saved;
28 for the Lord will execute His word on the land, thoroughly and quickly."
29 And just as Isaiah foretold, "Unless the Lord of Sabaoth had left to us a seed, We would have become like Sodom, and would have resembled Gomorrah."

Paul turns to Hosea and Isaiah to show that Gentile inclusion and Jewish preservation were always part of God's plan. God calls those who were not His people. God preserves a remnant by grace. His word has not failed.

Israel's Stumbling

Romans 9:30–33

30 What shall we say then? That Gentiles, who did not pursue righteousness, laid hold of righteousness, even the righteousness which is by faith;
31 but Israel, pursuing a law of righteousness, did not attain that law.
32 Why? Because they did not pursue it by faith, but as though it were by works.
33 "The one who believes upon Him will not be put to shame."

Christ is either a sanctuary or a stumbling stone. Everything turns on faith.

Stepping Forward

These truths are not presented as abstract ideas. As Paul unfolds them, they press directly on how God's mercy is understood and trusted, particularly when His ways challenge human expectations.

With the overall movement of Paul's argument now in view, we are ready to slow our pace and examine the text with more detail. We now begin where he begins: with sorrow for Israel. Paul's grief, love, and concern for his own people frame everything that follows and must be heard before his arguments, warnings, and conclusions can be rightly understood.

CHAPTER 1

2

Chapter 2

The Identity of Paul's Kinsmen According to the Flesh

Romans 9:3–5

Paul opens this section with staggering grief, so deep it almost defies comprehension. He speaks not as a detached theologian, but as a man whose heart is bound to his people. Before Paul explains anything about God's purposes, he allows us to see the personal cost those purposes carry for him.

His words are not rhetorical. He is expressing real anguish. If it were possible, he says, he would bear separation from Christ if it meant the salvation of his own people. This is not a doctrinal exaggeration; it is the cry of a shepherd's heart.

Yet Paul is not suggesting that such a sacrifice could actually save Israel. Only Christ can do that. What Paul is doing is revealing the depth of his love and preparing the reader for the question that now presses inescapably forward.

If Israel has rejected her Messiah, has God failed to keep His promises?

That question governs everything that follows in Romans 9–11.

The Text

3 For I could wish that I myself were accursed, separated from Christ for the sake of my brothers, my kinsmen according to the flesh,
4 who are Israelites, to whom belongs the adoption as sons, and the glory and the covenants and the giving of the Law and the temple service and the promises,
5 whose are the fathers, and from whom is the Christ according to the flesh, who is God over all, blessed forever. Amen.

Who Are Paul's "Kinsmen According to the Flesh"?

In verse 3, Paul identifies those for whom he grieves as his "kinsmen according to the flesh." By this phrase, he is speaking of ethnic Israelites—the physical descendants of Abraham through Isaac and Jacob. The wording is precise. "According to the flesh" identifies lineage, not spiritual standing. Paul is not redefining Israel here; he is naming her plainly.

13

The identity of Israel itself traces back to a defining moment in redemptive history, which is established in Genesis 32:28.

Genesis 32:24–28
24 Then Jacob was left alone, and a man wrestled with him until the breaking of dawn.
25 And he saw that he had not prevailed against him, so he touched the socket of his thigh, and the socket of Jacob's thigh was dislocated while he wrestled with him.
26 Then he said, "Let me go, for the dawn is breaking." But he said, "I will not let you go unless you bless me."
27 So he said to him, "What is your name?" And he said, "Jacob."
28 Then He said, "Your name shall no longer be Jacob, but Israel; for you have striven with God and with men and have prevailed."

From that moment forward, Israel existed as a people marked by God's covenant relationship—formed through promise, preserved through mercy, and often struggling in faithfulness. Some believed. Many did not. But God's covenant purposes toward them remained intact.

This distinction matters. Physical descent never guaranteed salvation; unbelief, however, never nullified God's promises. Paul will spend the rest of these chapters carefully holding both truths together.

Israel and the Church: Distinct, Yet Related

Throughout Romans 9–11, Paul consistently uses *Israel* to mean ethnic Israel. The church, by contrast, is composed of believing Jews and believing Gentiles united in Christ.

Believing Jews are part of the church.

Believing Gentiles are grafted in.

But Israel is not absorbed into the church, nor is Israel redefined as a symbolic or purely spiritual idea.

God's redemptive plan includes both Israel and The Church, each with a distinct role in the unfolding story.

The Privileged Identity of Israel

In verses 4 and 5, Paul lists Israel's extraordinary privileges—not to exalt Israel, but to intensify the weight of her unbelief.

To Israel belonged adoption, glory, covenants, the Law, temple worship, and the promises. These were not incidental blessings, but deliberate gifts through which God carried His purposes forward in history.

They were descended from the patriarchs—Abraham, Isaac, and Jacob—men to whom God personally bound Himself by oath.

And then Paul names the greatest privilege of all.

The Final and Greatest Privilege: Christ Came From Israel

Paul's language shifts deliberately.

Everything else is introduced with *to whom belongs*.

But when Paul speaks of Christ, he writes *from whom*.

Christ did not belong to Israel as a possession.

He came **through** Israel as a gift to the world.

Jesus is Jewish according to the flesh.

He ministered first among the Jewish people.

He fulfilled Israel's Scriptures.

And yet He is God over all, blessed forever.

This distinction matters. Christ's origin does not limit His reach. Salvation flows outward from Israel to the nations, but it does not erase Israel from the story.

3

Chapter 3

God's Covenant Faithfulness Clarified

Romans 9:6–9

Paul now addresses directly the question that presses beneath his grief. In light of Israel's widespread unbelief, he asks what every careful reader must ask: **has the word of God failed?**

The Text

6 But it is not as though the word of God has failed. For they are not all Israel who are descended from Israel;
7 nor are they all children because they are Abraham's seed, but, "Through Isaac your seed will be named."
8 That is, the children of the flesh are not the children of God,

but the children of the promise are regarded as seed.

9 For this is the word of promise: "At this time I will come, and Sarah shall have a son."

Verse 6: God's Word Has Not Failed

Paul begins in verse 6 with a decisive clarification: *"It is not as though the word of God has failed."* His answer is immediate and unqualified. No. The problem does not lie with God's promise, but with a misunderstanding of how that promise has always operated.

Still in verse 6, Paul introduces a careful distinction that governs everything that follows: *"For they are not all Israel who are descended from Israel."* Belonging to Israel physically has never been identical to belonging to Israel in the sense of receiving God's saving promises. Paul is not redefining Israel; he is explaining how God has always worked within Israel.

There has always been a distinction between physical descent and covenant fulfillment—between those who belong to Israel by lineage and those who belong to Israel by promise.

Verse 7: Physical Descent Was Never Sufficient

In verse 7, Paul sharpens the distinction he has already introduced:

7"Nor are they all children because they are Abraham's seed."

Physical descent from Abraham was never, by itself, the basis of covenant fulfillment. Lineage alone did not guarantee participation in the promise. Paul anchors this claim directly in Scripture: "Through Isaac your seed will be named."

This was not a later theological adjustment, nor a response to Israel's present unbelief. It was God's stated intention from the beginning. Long before Isaac was born, God promised Abraham that the covenant would pass through him:

Genesis 21:12
12 "Through Isaac your seed shall be named."

Abraham had other sons. Ishmael was also his biological descendant. Yet God Himself drew the lineage of promise— not according to natural order, cultural expectation, or human reasoning, but by His own promise.

By pointing to Isaac, Paul reminds his readers that the distinction he is making did not arise in response to Christ or to Israel's unbelief, but was established long before, at the beginning of God's covenant dealings.

Verse 8: Flesh and Promise Distinguished

Verse 8 draws the conclusion explicitly: *"That is, the children of the flesh are not the children of God, but the children of the promise are regarded as seed."* Here Paul names the distinction directly.

Some are connected to Abraham by physical descent; others are counted as his true offspring because God has promised to make them so. The difference is not effort, merit, or heritage, but God's call. Belonging to God's people has never rested on who one is born from, but on whom God chooses to act for. From the beginning, covenant identity has been established by promise received, not lineage possessed

This verse makes clear that Paul is not introducing two different peoples of God. He is clarifying a distinction that has always existed within Israel itself—between physical descent and saving promise.

Verse 9: The Promise Creates What It Commands

In verse 9, Paul grounds the entire argument in God's own words:

"For this is the word of promise: 'At this time I will come, and Sarah shall have a son.'"

This promise reaches back to Genesis itself:

Genesis 18:10
10 "I will surely return to you at this time next year; and behold, Sarah your wife will have a son."

After Isaac's birth, God confirmed that the covenant line would be defined by promise, not by mere biology. Isaac's birth was not the result of human planning or ability. It was the result of divine intervention at an appointed time. God spoke, and life followed. The promise did not respond to circumstances; it created what it required.

This is the pattern Paul wants the reader to see. God's promises do not merely identify who will be saved; they create the people they name. Those whom God elects, He also calls.

What Is Really at Stake

Paul's statement in verse 6 is not a passing remark. It marks a decisive turning point in his argument, and it only makes sense if more than national identity is at stake. Paul is not merely asking whether Israel still has a place in God's plan. He is confronting a far deeper question: whether God remains faithful to His saving promises when many within Israel are rejecting Christ, even as Gentiles—once outside those promises—are now believing the gospel.

Here one truth must remain clearly in view: **Paul is tracing the faithfulness of God's promise, not the failure of human response.**

Some readers want to resolve the tension quickly by saying that Romans 9 concerns only God's choice of Israel as a nation. There is truth in that claim, but it is not the whole truth. God unquestionably chose Israel as His covenant nation and entrusted her with the covenants, the Law, the promises, and ultimately the Messiah. Paul affirms this without hesitation. Yet Romans 9 presses further, because national election alone cannot explain why some within Israel believe while others do not, nor how God's saving promises remain faithful in the face of widespread unbelief.

At the same time, Paul is not choosing between two competing ideas. Scripture consistently presents both God's covenant choice of Israel as a nation and His gracious choice of a believing remnant within that nation. These realities operate together throughout redemptive history.

National election alone does not explain the objections Paul anticipates later in the chapter:

Is God unjust?
  Why does He still find fault?

Those questions do not arise from national privilege or historical role. They arise only when God's mercy and judgment are understood to be applied at the level of individual salvation.

An Israel Within Israel

In Romans 9:6–9, Paul shows that God's covenant promises have not failed the nation of Israel because God's saving plan was never aimed at every individual within the nation without distinction. From the very beginning, God was working through a believing remnant within Israel—**an Israel within Israel**.

There were Israelites who belonged to Abraham by physical descent.

There were Israelites who belonged to God by faith. Both were part of the nation. Not all were part of the promise.

Behind all of these distinctions stands one faithful God, full of mercy, whose saving intention has never failed. God has not failed His people Israel. From the very beginning, God's saving work has moved through a remnant, those sustained by His promise rather than by physical descent alone.

Preparing for What Comes Next

A thoughtful reader may still wonder whether another explanation remains. Perhaps Isaac was chosen simply because he was Sarah's child. Perhaps the distinction still rests, in some way, on circumstance or birth.

Paul anticipates that question.

And in the next movement of his argument, he removes it entirely. He will move from Abraham's sons to Isaac's twins—Jacob and Esau. They share the same parents. They are conceived at the same moment. Neither has acted. Neither has earned anything.

Paul does not rush us there. He prepares us. He wants every familiar explanation gently set aside so that when he speaks of God's sovereign call, we are not startled by it, but ready to receive it with humility and trust.

This is where Paul's careful explanation now moves forward.

4

Chapter 4

Paul Continues to Strengthen His Case for Election

Romans 9:10–13

Having shown in Romans 9:6–9 that God's promises have always operated according to His choosing rather than mere physical descent, Paul anticipates a remaining hesitation a reader might have.

The difference between Isaac and Ishmael could still seem easy to explain in human terms. Ishmael was born to Hagar, Sarah's servant. She bore Abraham a son, but she was not his wife in the way Sarah was. Isaac, on the other hand, was born to Sarah, Abraham's wife and the woman God had specifically promised would bear the child of the covenant. Because of this, it would be natural to think the distinction rests on family order or social standing, rather than on God's promise itself.

Paul does not ignore that lingering thought. Nor does he argue around it. Instead, he moves the discussion forward deliberately by stepping down one generation. If birth, lineage, or legitimacy were the true reason for God's choice, then once those factors are held equal, no remaining difference should exist.

So Paul turns to Isaac's own household and asks us to look closely at his sons, Jacob and Esau—two children with the same father and the same mother, conceived at the same moment, sharing the same lineage and inheritance. No difference in ethnicity. No difference in legitimacy. No difference in opportunity.

By placing these two brothers side by side, Paul removes the last remaining human explanation a reader might appeal to. He is not multiplying examples for effect, but narrowing the field until only one explanation remains: God's sovereign purpose.

The Text

10 And not only this, but there was Rebekah also, when she had conceived twins by one man, our father Isaac;
11 for though the twins were not yet born and had not done anything good or bad, so that the purpose of God according to His choice would stand, not because of works but because of Him who calls,
12 it was said to her, "The older shall serve the younger."
13 Just as it is written, "Jacob I loved, but Esau I hated."

Verse 10: One Father, One Mother, One Conception

Paul's opening words in verse 10 — "And not only this" — signal that he is adding further proof to what he has already established. He knows objections remain, and he addresses them directly rather than defensively.

By noting that Rebekah conceived twins "by one man, our father Isaac," Paul deliberately removes every possible distinction of lineage. He speaks as a Jew to fellow Jews, grounding the argument in Israel's own family history. This is not an abstract theological example; it is the shared story of their fathers.

The emphasis is clear: the conditions are now equal.

Verse 11: God's Purpose Precedes Human Action

Verse 11 identifies the controlling reason behind God's choice, and Paul places it before anything else is allowed to speak.

"Though the twins were not yet born and had not done anything good or bad..."

Paul eliminates merit entirely. No deeds. No character. No foreseen action.

Why?

"So that the purpose of God according to His choice would stand, not because of works but because of Him who calls."

Here Paul states the principle explicitly. God's saving purpose rests on His call, not on human effort, foreseen faith, or moral distinction. The choice is made before history unfolds so that its true source cannot be mistaken.

This is the heart of Paul's argument. God's word has not failed because His promises were never grounded in what human beings would do, but in what God had already purposed to do.

Verse 12: God Speaks Before They Act

In verse 12, Paul reminds us that God's declaration came before the twins were born:

"It was said to her, 'The older shall serve the younger.'"

Paul is quoting Genesis 25:23, where the Lord spoke to Rebekah while the children were still in her womb:

Genesis 25:23

23 And Yahweh said to her, "Two nations are in your womb; And two peoples will be separated from your body; And one people shall be stronger than the other; And the older shall serve the younger."

This declaration was not a reaction. It was not a response to behavior. It was a sovereign declaration of purpose.

Paul is showing that God's word does not wait for history to justify it. It establishes history according to God's design.

Verse 13: Scripture Interprets Scripture

Paul's statement in verse 13, "Jacob I loved, but Esau I hated", comes from the prophet Malachi. Paul is not importing a new interpretation into Israel's story, but allowing Scripture to interpret Scripture.

Malachi 1:2–3
2 "I have loved you," says Yahweh.
"But you say, 'How have You loved us?'
'Was not Esau Jacob's brother?' declares Yahweh.
'Yet I have loved Jacob;
3 but I have hated Esau…'"

Malachi is not describing fluctuating emotions. He is interpreting God's covenant actions over time. God's love for Jacob is displayed in His choosing and preserving Israel. God's hatred of Esau is displayed in His decision to pass him over and withhold covenant blessing.

Love and hate here are covenantal actions, not emotional volatility. Jacob was chosen to inherit the promises. Esau was passed over, not because of works, but because of God's sovereign purpose.

God's Purpose According to His Choice

Romans 9:11 makes the governing principle unmistakable: God's purpose stands because of Him who calls, not because of works.

Neither brother deserved mercy. Both were sinners by nature. Yet God's choice was unconditional and grounded entirely in His sovereign grace.

This pattern echoes across Scripture. God saves and calls according to His own purpose, not according to human effort. His choice precedes faith and produces faith.

Election does not diminish responsibility, nor does it excuse sin. It magnifies mercy. Jacob received grace he did not deserve. Esau received justice, which God is never obligated to withhold.

A Necessary Moment of Reflection

At this point, Scripture invites us to slow down, not to soften what Paul has said, but to let it register.

Paul is not asking us to determine who belongs to God, nor to speculate beyond what has been revealed. He is tracing how God has always worked and asking us to reckon honestly with where salvation truly begins.

If this teaching feels weighty, that reaction is understandable. Paul is not skimming the surface here. He is pressing into something that touches the heart of the gospel itself: whether salvation ultimately depends on us, on who we are, what we bring, or how well we respond, or whether it rests entirely on God's mercy from beginning to end.

Seen this way, election is not meant to unsettle faith, but to steady it. It does not stand in competition with the free offer of the gospel; it helps us understand why that offer truly saves. If salvation depended on human distinction, it would always be fragile. But because it rests on God's mercy, it is secure.

The God who chooses is the same God who invites sinners to repent, who shows compassion freely, and who keeps hold of those He saves. Paul is not pulling the ground out from under faith. He is showing us what that ground is made of.

5

Chapter 5

Is God Unfair?

Romans 9:14–18

As Paul moves into Romans 9:14–18, he is responding directly to the tension his argument has created. He has shown that God's saving purpose operates according to His sovereign choice rather than human descent, effort, or merit. God chose Isaac, not Ishmael. He chose Jacob, not Esau. And He did so before either had done anything good or bad, so that His purpose according to election would stand.

Paul knows the objection this raises immediately. If God's mercy is sovereign and His choice precedes human action, then a serious charge presses to the surface.

Is God unjust?

Paul does not dismiss that question or treat it lightly. He brings it into the open and answers it directly. Paul answers this charge in a deliberate way, moving step by step to show that God's mercy and justice are not in conflict, but perfectly aligned.

The Text

14 What shall we say then? Is there any unrighteousness with God? May it never be!
15 For He says to Moses, "I will have mercy on whom I have mercy, and I will have compassion on whom I have compassion."
16 So then it does not depend on the one who wills or the one who runs, but on God who has mercy.
17 For the Scripture says to Pharaoh, "For this very purpose I raised you up, to demonstrate My power in you, and that My name might be proclaimed throughout the whole earth."
18 So then He has mercy on whom He desires, and He hardens whom He desires.

Movement One: Paul Vindicates God's Righteousness

Romans 9:14

Paul begins in verse 14 by voicing the objection himself: *"What shall we say then? Is there any unrighteousness with God?"*

He answers with the strongest possible denial: *"May it never be!"*

The charge itself is unthinkable. There is no unrighteousness with God, not even the smallest trace.

At this point, Paul reframes the question. Justice is often defined as giving each person what they deserve. But Paul presses deeper by forcing us to ask a prior question: What does God deserve? What is owed to Him by His creatures?

Scripture consistently answers that God is owed honor, gratitude, worship, and glory. The fundamental human problem is not that God withholds mercy, but that humanity refuses to give God what He is due.

As Isaiah records in Isaiah 48:11:
11 "For My own sake, for My own sake, I will act;
For how can My name be profaned?
And My glory I will not give to another."
Paul has already established this diagnosis earlier in Romans:

Romans 1:21–23
21 For even though they knew God, they did not honor Him as God or give thanks, but they became futile in their thoughts, and their foolish heart was darkened.
22 Professing to be wise, they became fools,
23 and exchanged the glory of the incorruptible God for an image.

Paul invites us to consider that the deepest injustice may not be that God shows mercy selectively, but that fallen humanity treats the glory of God as though it were of little worth. God would be unrighteous if He failed to uphold His own glory.

This prepares us for how Paul answers the charge, not by appealing to human standards of fairness, but by appealing to

God's revealed character.

Movement Two: God Displays His Glory Through Sovereign Mercy

Romans 9:15–16

In verses 15–16, Paul grounds his answer in Scripture itself by quoting God's own words to Moses:

"I will have mercy on whom I have mercy, and I will have compassion on whom I have compassion."

This quotation comes from Exodus 33:19, spoken in the aftermath of Israel's golden calf rebellion. Israel had committed blatant idolatry, exchanging the glory of God for a lifeless image. Strict justice would have meant their destruction.

Instead, God revealed His glory by declaring His sovereign freedom to show mercy.

Exodus 33:18–19
18 Then Moses said, "I pray You, show me Your glory!"
19 And He said, "I Myself will make all My goodness pass before you, and will proclaim the name of Yahweh before you; and I will be gracious to whom I will be gracious, and will show compassion on whom I will show compassion."

Paul's logic is deliberate. God reveals His glory not by submitting to human expectations or demands, but by asserting His sovereign freedom. Mercy, by definition, cannot be demanded. If mercy were owed, it would no longer be mercy.

Paul draws the conclusion explicitly in verse 16:

"So then it does not depend on the one who wills or the one who runs, but on God who has mercy."

Salvation does not rest on human decision or effort. It rests on God's gracious will.

Clarifying Justice and Mercy

Here Paul forces us to think carefully. Scripture emphasizes **retributive justice**—giving what is earned. Justice sends sinners to judgment. Mercy gives what is not earned.

Modern assumptions often import **distributive justice** into salvation, arguing that God must give mercy equally to all. But Scripture never defines mercy that way. God owes justice; He owes mercy to no one.

If mercy were required by justice, it would cease to be mercy altogether.

This reframes the question. The question is not, *Why doesn't God show mercy to everyone?*

The real question is, *Why does God show mercy to anyone at all?*

Movement Three: God Displays His Glory Through Righteous Judgment

Romans 9:17–18

In verses 17–18, Paul turns to a second Old Testament example—Pharaoh.

"For the Scripture says to Pharaoh..."

Paul is quoting **Exodus 9:16**, where God explains why Pharaoh's rule and resistance were allowed to continue.

Exodus 9:14–16

14 "For this time I will send all My plagues against your heart and against your servants and your people, so that you may know that there is no one like Me in all the earth.

15 For if by now I had sent forth My hand and struck you and your people with pestilence, you would then have been wiped out from the earth.

16 But indeed, for this reason I have caused you to stand, in order to show you My power and to recount My name through all the earth."

God could have destroyed Egypt immediately. Instead, He prolonged Pharaoh's rebellion so that His power and glory would be unmistakably displayed.

Scripture carefully holds two truths together:

- Pharaoh hardened his own heart.
- God judicially hardened Pharaoh by withholding mercy and confirming him in his rebellion.

Pharaoh's own words reveal his posture:

Exodus 5:2
2 "Who is Yahweh that I should obey His voice...? I do not know Yahweh..."

Pharaoh acts freely according to his sinful nature. God remains sovereign, patiently directing even human rebellion to serve His righteous purpose.

Exodus 7:3–5
3 "I will harden Pharaoh's heart..."
5 "And the Egyptians shall know that I am Yahweh..."

Paul's conclusion in verse 18 is unavoidable:
18 *"So then He has mercy on whom He desires, and He hardens whom He desires."*

In neither case is God unjust. Mercy is undeserved. Judgment is deserved.

A Necessary Bridge: Mercy, Judgment, and the Cross

At this point, a thoughtful reader may feel the weight of what Paul is saying and quietly wonder how mercy can be righteous. Paul does not answer that question here , not because it is unimportant, but because it has already been answered. Earlier in Romans, Paul made clear that God never sets justice aside to show mercy. He satisfies justice fully, so that mercy may be given freely. That foundation remains in place as Paul presses forward.

2 Corinthians 5:21
21 He made Him who knew no sin to be sin on our behalf...

Romans 3:25–26
25–26 God displayed Christ as a propitiation... so that He would be just and the justifier...

Mercy and justice do not compete. They meet.

Preparing for What Comes Next

Paul knows the discussion is not finished. If God's mercy is sovereign and His choice decisive, then another question presses forward:

What responsibility remains for the human creature?

Paul does not evade that question. He allows it to stand, because it exposes something deeper than theology—the posture of the human heart before its Creator.

Romans 9:19–23 does not retreat from the truth already stated.

It presses further into it.

6

Chapter 6

The Potter's Freedom

Romans 9:19–24

Having demonstrated that God's word has not failed, Paul has shown that God's saving promises have never rested on physical descent or human effort, but on His sovereign purpose in election. From Isaac rather than Ishmael, and Jacob rather than Esau, God's choice precedes birth, works, and merit, standing solely on His call. He is free to bestow mercy on whom He wills and righteous to harden those who persist in rebellion, as seen in His dealings with both Israel and Pharaoh. Grace is never owed, judgment is never unjust, and God's glory is displayed in both mercy and justice, even when that glory challenges our natural instincts.

Yet Paul knows this teaching presses directly against human pride and natural reasoning, and he does not pretend otherwise. If God sovereignly chooses and hardens, how can He still hold anyone responsible? It is this objection—one that challenges the creature's posture before the Creator—that Paul now addresses.

The Text

19 You will say to me then, "Why does He still find fault? For who resists His will?"

20 On the contrary, who are you, O man, who answers back to God? Will the thing molded say to the molder, "Why did you make me like this"?

21 Or does not the potter have authority over the clay, to make from the same lump one vessel for honorable use and another for dishonorable use?

22 And what if God, wanting to demonstrate His wrath and to make His power known, endured with much patience vessels of wrath having been prepared for destruction,

23 and in order that He might make known the riches of His glory upon vessels of mercy, which He prepared beforehand for glory—

24 even us, whom He also called, not from among Jews only, but also from among Gentiles?

The Creature Confronted by the Creator

Romans 9:19–20

Paul anticipates the objection that inevitably arises once God's sovereign mercy and hardening are clearly stated.

Verse 19 gives voice to the protest. If God's will is decisive, how can He still hold anyone accountable? The objection is logically consistent with fallen human reasoning, and it is a question many thoughtful readers quietly carry. Paul does not deny the premise. God's will cannot be thwarted. What he confronts is the conclusion drawn from it, and the posture behind the question itself.

Verse 20 shifts the ground entirely. Paul does not begin with philosophical explanation. He begins with reorientation. The issue is not merely logic; it is posture. We are creatures. God is Creator.

Scripture consistently affirms this defining distinction.

Isaiah 46:9–10
9 "Remember the former things of old; for I am God, and there is no other;
10 I am God, and there is none like Me, declaring the end from the beginning… My counsel shall stand, and I will do all My pleasure."

Psalm 115:3
3 "But our God is in the heavens; He does whatever He pleases."

Paul insists on three truths that Scripture holds together without apology:

1. God is absolutely sovereign.
2. Human beings remain morally responsible.
3. Our inability to fully harmonize these truths does not make either one less true

The objection itself reveals the deeper issue. The word *resists* implies ongoing defiance, meaning setting the human will against the will of God. This is not neutral inquiry. It is answering back to God.

Paul draws a firm boundary, not to silence honest struggle, but to remind us who we are and who God is. God is not obligated to explain Himself to His creatures. He is accountable to no one. We are accountable to Him.

The Potter and the Clay: God's Sovereign Authority

Romans 9:20

Paul introduces an intentionally absurd image to expose human presumption. Clay protesting its potter is meant to sound as irrational as it is irreverent. The image is not designed to humiliate us, but to humble us and to reestablish the proper relationship between Creator and creature.

When Paul speaks of "the thing molded," he is describing something entirely formed by another. The language emphasizes dependence, not autonomy. The clay does not define itself, direct itself, or explain itself. It only even exists because the potter acts to create it. Paul writes:

20 "Will the thing molded say to the molder, 'Why did you make me like this?'

The imagery Paul uses immediately echoes the creation account itself.

Genesis 2:7

7 "Then Yahweh God formed man of dust from the ground, and breathed into his nostrils the breath of life; and man became a living soul."

From the beginning, humanity is not self-originating or self-determining. We exist by God's creative will and remain accountable to Him. Scripture consistently affirms that God alone is the Former, and we are the formed.

The Same Lump and God's Distinct Purposes

Romans 9:21
Paul then states the distinction explicitly.

21 "Does not the potter have authority over the clay, to make from the same lump one vessel for honorable use and another for dishonorable use?"

Paul grounds everything that follows in this Creator–creature distinction. From the same fallen humanity, God forms:

- vessels for honorable use—objects of mercy, prepared for glory
- vessels for dishonorable use—objects of wrath, fitted for destruction

The phrase *the same lump* matters greatly. When Paul speaks of "the same lump," he is not describing humanity as it was at creation, but humanity as it exists after the fall—sinful,

43

guilty, and descended from Adam. God was not working with innocent clay, but with fallen humanity already in need of either mercy or judgment.

God, knowing from eternity that Adam would fall and that humanity would exist as a fallen race, **permitted that fall within His sovereign purpose** and purposed to show mercy to some from that fallen humanity, not because of anything in them, but according to His gracious will. God is not creating moral difference where none existed. He is dealing with a humanity already guilty and already in need.

This is where Scripture makes a careful and essential distinction. **Election** is a positive act of mercy. God actively intervenes to rescue sinners who would never rescue themselves. **Reprobation** is a negative act of judgment. God passes over sinners and leaves them in the path they have chosen.

These are not symmetrical acts. Scripture speaks this way not to provoke speculation, but to preserve what must be held together: God's perfect goodness and His absolute sovereignty. God saves actively. He judges justly. He is the author of salvation, not the author of sin.

Paul then shows that this principle is not theoretical. It is demonstrated in real history.

Pharaoh serves as a case study of **judicial hardening applied to the same fallen lump**. God did not create Pharaoh's rebellion. He judicially hardened a man already in rebellion, confirming him in the path he had freely chosen. Pharaoh was not forced into defiance; he was handed over to it.

Exodus 9:16
16 "But indeed, for this reason I have caused you to stand, in order to show you My power and to recount My name through

all the earth."

God could have ended Pharaoh's rule immediately. Instead, He endured Pharaoh's rebellion so that His power and His name would be made known. This hardening was purposeful, patient, and righteous.

Scripture repeatedly affirms God's absolute authority over all creatures and all events.

Daniel 4:35
35 "All the inhabitants of the earth are reputed as nothing;
    But He does according to His will...
    And no one can strike against His hand or say to Him, 'What have You done?'"

Even Job, after wrestling deeply with God, ultimately fell silent before this reality.

Job 40:4
4 "Behold, I am insignificant; what shall I reply to You? I put my hand on my mouth."

Paul is calling for a posture not of intellectual surrender, but of reverent humility. He is not asking us to stop thinking or wrestling with hard truths. He is calling us to recognize the limits of the creature before the Creator. Faith grows not by forcing God into our categories, but by trusting Him where our understanding reaches its edge.

God's Purpose: Displaying His Glory in Wrath and Mercy

Romans 9:22–24

Not only does Paul rebuke finite man for answering back in verses 19–21, but verses 22–23 come as close as anywhere in Scripture to explaining why God does not extend saving mercy to all—not by opening His hidden counsel, but by revealing what He has chosen to make known about His purposes.

22 "And what if God, wanting to demonstrate His wrath and to make His power known, endured with much patience vessels of wrath having been prepared for destruction,

23 and in order that He might make known the riches of His glory upon vessels of mercy, which He prepared beforehand for glory—"

Paul draws our attention to what God desires to make known. God's glory is not a single attribute but the full display of His divine perfections. In enduring vessels of wrath with patience, God demonstrates His justice, power, and restraint. Judgment remains real and deserved, yet God does not act impulsively or hastily.

By contrast, vessels of mercy are not merely spared judgment; they are intentionally prepared for glory. Mercy is active, deliberate, and gracious.

Those who receive wrath receive what justice demands.

Those who receive mercy receive what grace supplies.

The deeper question, then, is not *Why does God judge sinners?*

but *Why does God save any at all?* Paul's answer is clear: God shows mercy in order to make known the riches of His glory. Romans 9:24

24 "Even us, whom He also called, not from among Jews only, but also from among Gentiles."

God's mercy was never narrow. The same sovereign grace that preserved a remnant within Israel now reaches beyond Israel, gathering a people from the nations. God's redemptive purpose has always been global, gracious, and glory-centered.

Preparing for What Comes Next

Paul has now pressed us to the edge of what it means to be a creature before a sovereign God. He has not diminished human responsibility, nor has he softened divine sovereignty. He has allowed both to stand in their full force.

What Paul has shown so far is demanding, but it is not the whole picture. The same Scriptures that speak plainly about God's sovereignty will now show us the wideness of His mercy and the patience of His saving purpose.

The next question will not be abstract. It will be deeply personal.

If God acts this way, what responsibility remains for us?

Paul will not retreat from the truth already stated. He will press further into it, continuing to speak plainly, but never carelessly, as he leads us forward.

Romans 9:25–29 will show that none of this is new. The

prophets themselves declared it long ago.

Chapter 7

Vessels of Mercy: Unlikely Converts

Romans 9:25-29

Every Christian is an unlikely convert to Christ. No one becomes a believer because they were naturally inclined toward God, spiritually perceptive, or morally prepared. God makes Christians because God's grace operates according to God's choice. That is why Paul has described believers throughout this chapter as *"vessels of mercy."* Every Christian is a living display of undeserved grace.

Paul has already shown that God's purpose in election has always been to create a people for Himself, not on the basis of physical descent, human effort, or merit, but according to His sovereign mercy. Within Israel, that purpose has taken the form of a preserved remnant. Beyond Israel, it now extends to people drawn from every tribe, tongue, and nation.

In verses 19–24, Paul confronted the natural human objection to God's sovereignty. If God is truly sovereign, how can He still hold anyone accountable? Paul did not answer by softening God's sovereignty or adjusting divine justice to human expectations. Instead, he reoriented us. God is the Potter; we are the clay. He is not accountable to His creation, and yet He is never unjust.

Paul then explained that God patiently endures vessels of wrath, not because He delights in judgment, but because He is accomplishing a greater purpose. Through patience, God makes His power known. More importantly, He does so in order to make known the riches of His glory upon vessels of mercy—people He prepared beforehand for glory.

That truth sets the stage for what comes next. Having shown *how* God acts as sovereign Potter, Paul now turns to Scripture to show *who* those vessels of mercy are, and *where* they come from.

God's Promises Confirmed by the Prophets

Paul makes a closing move in this section. He does not introduce a new doctrine; he confirms what he has already argued by appealing to the Old Testament. If God's saving purpose truly operates this way, then it should not surprise us when Scripture itself bears witness to it.

Paul supports his case with two prophetic voices:

- Hosea, to show the surprising inclusion of those once called *"not My people"*

- Isaiah, to show the sobering reality that only a remnant of Israel would be saved

Together, these prophecies show that God's promises have not failed. They are being fulfilled exactly as foretold.

The Text

25 As He says also in Hosea, "I will call those who were not My people, 'My people,' And her who was not beloved, 'beloved.'"
26 "And it shall be that in the place where it was said to them, 'You are not My people,' There they shall be called sons of the living God."
27 And Isaiah cries out concerning Israel, "Though the number of the sons of Israel be like the sand of the sea, It is the remnant that will be saved;
28 For the Lord will execute His word on the land, thoroughly and quickly."
29 And just as Isaiah foretold, "Unless the Lord of Sabaoth had left to us a seed, We would have become like Sodom, And would have resembled Gomorrah."

Paul is not lifting isolated phrases. He is drawing from whole prophetic contexts his readers would have known—and that context matters.

Hosea: God Calls the Unlikely

In verses 25 and 26, Paul begins with Hosea because Hosea's message most directly explains the surprising inclusion of outsiders.

In Hosea's day, Israel stood under covenant discipline. As part of his prophetic ministry, God commanded Hosea to give his own children names that publicly declared Israel's condition:

- Jezreel, announcing judgment and scattering
- Lo-Ruhamah, meaning "No mercy"
- Lo-Ammi, meaning "Not my people"

Hosea's children's names made Israel's situation unmistakable. Through them, God publicly declared that the nation stood under judgment, cut off from covenant blessing, and described by God Himself as no longer His people.

Yet judgment was not the final word. Hosea also proclaimed a future reversal—a sovereign act of mercy in which God would reclaim those He had disciplined. The very people once labeled *"not My people"* would be renamed and restored by grace.

Hosea declared that those once called *"not My people"* would be called *sons of the living God.*

This is the language Paul quotes in Romans 9:25–26. His point is steady and clear: God has always possessed the authority to create a people where there appeared to be none. He renames. He restores. He calls.

In Hosea's day, this promise spoke first to Israel under discipline. But Paul, writing under the inspiration of the Spirit, shows its broader reach. If God can take those once called *"not*

My people" and make them His people, then He is free to gather Gentile sinners into His covenant mercy as well.

This matters because Romans 9 is not merely explaining a doctrine; it is defending God's faithfulness. God's promises have not failed. The prophets themselves said He would call the unlikely.

Isaiah: A Remnant Preserved by Mercy

Now in verses 27-29, Paul turns to Isaiah—not to repeat Hosea's point, but to balance it.

If God's mercy can reach outward to those once excluded, what about Israel itself?

Isaiah answers that question.

Paul quotes Isaiah to show that Israel's present condition should not surprise us. Even when Israel was numerically vast, salvation was never promised to the nation as a whole. God preserved His purposes through a remnant, kept not by entitlement, but by mercy.

Isaiah declared in 10:22–23
22 For though your people, O Israel, may be like the sand of the sea,
    Only a remnant within them will return;
    A destruction is determined, overflowing with righteousness.
23 For a complete destruction, one that is decreed,
    The Lord Yahweh of hosts will execute in the midst of all the

land.

The promise was never that every descendant of Abraham would be saved. Even when Israel's numbers were vast—"like the sand of the sea"—it would be the remnant that would return. Salvation would come through a smaller, preserved people, not through national size or heritage.

Paul then adds a second quotation, pressing the point even further, which he takes from Isaiah 1:9:

9 Unless Yahweh of hosts had left us a seed, We would have become like Sodom, And would have been like Gomorrah.

Here Isaiah makes the implication unmistakable. Israel's continued existence as a people of promise was not owed to them. Without God's merciful intervention—without Him leaving a "seed"—Israel would have been completely destroyed, indistinguishable from cities judged for their wickedness.

Paul's use of Isaiah is deliberately focused. He is not unfolding every dimension of Isaiah's prophecy. He is making one clear and essential point: Israel's history has always been sustained by mercy, not by guarantee. The existence of a believing remnant is not evidence that God's promises have failed, but that His mercy has prevailed.

Taken together, Hosea and Isaiah establish two truths that stand side by side:

- God freely calls those who were once outside His people
- God mercifully preserves a remnant within Israel

Both realities confirm the same conclusion Paul has been

defending from the start: God's word has not failed.

A Brief Bridge Forward

At this point, Paul has accomplished what this section requires. He has shown that the present shape of God's people—Gentiles being gathered in, Israel represented by a remnant—is not an accident, a detour, or a contradiction of God's promises. It is the outworking of what God declared long ago.

This passage does not yet answer every question about Israel's future, nor is it meant to. Its purpose is more immediate and more pastoral: to steady the reader's confidence in God's faithfulness.

God's purposes do not hang on numbers, heritage, or human consistency. They rest on mercy.

For the believer, this truth is meant to bring reassurance, not anxiety. The same God who preserved a remnant then remains faithful to call, keep, and save His people in every generation.

Paul will continue to unfold these themes as he moves forward, but for now, Romans 9:25–29 leaves us with a settled confidence: God is doing exactly what He promised, even when His ways are unexpected.

8

Chapter 8

Zeal Without Submission

Romans 9:30–10:4

Up to this point, Paul has been answering one central, weight-bearing question: **Has God's saving word failed—and if not, who truly belongs to the people of God, and on what basis?**

He has shown that God's mercy reaches beyond Israel, yet does not include every Israelite without distinction. From the beginning, belonging to God's people has never rested on bloodline, effort, or religious privilege, but on God's merciful purpose and promise.

But Paul knows the next question presses in—especially for sincere, religious people.

If God is sovereign in salvation, why do some believe while others do not? And why has Israel, with all her privileges, largely rejected her Messiah?

Paul does not retreat from God's sovereignty, nor does he

excuse unbelief. Instead, he places divine mercy and human responsibility side by side. In Romans 9:30–10:4, Paul turns from God's eternal purpose to lived human response. Gentiles, who were not pursuing righteousness at all, received it by faith. Israel, who pursued righteousness intensely, failed to obtain it because they sought it in the wrong way.

This is not abstract theology for Paul. It is deeply personal. He speaks as a Jew who loves his people, prays for them, and grieves over their unbelief.

And Paul exposes a painful irony—one that remains just as present today:

It is possible to be deeply religious and yet miss the righteousness God freely gives

Scripture consistently warns that outward devotion, sincere effort, and even passionate service are not the same as knowing God. Jesus Himself spoke with sobering clarity about this danger.

Matthew 7:22–23

22 "Many will say to Me on that day, 'Lord, Lord, did we not prophesy in Your name, and in Your name cast out demons, and in Your name do many miracles?'

23 And then I will declare to them, 'I never knew you; depart from Me, you who practice lawlessness.'"

These are not people who rejected religion. They were immersed in it. They knew the language, performed the works, and assumed proximity to God meant acceptance by God. Yet they trusted in what they did *for* Him rather than resting in what He had done *for them*.

This is precisely the tragedy Paul is grieving in Romans 9–10.

Israel's failure was not a lack of zeal, sincerity, or effort. It was misplaced confidence. They pursued righteousness, but not by faith. They worked hard, but they would not submit. In the end, they trusted their obedience instead of receiving God's gift.

And that danger has never gone away.

The Text

30 What shall we say then? That Gentiles, who did not pursue righteousness, laid hold of righteousness, even the righteousness which is by faith;

31 but Israel, pursuing a law of righteousness, did not attain that law.

32 Why? Because they did not pursue it by faith, but as though it were by works. They stumbled over the stumbling stone,

33 just as it is written,

"Behold, I am laying in Zion a stone of stumbling and a rock of offense,

And the one who believes upon Him will not be put to shame."

10:1 Brothers, my heart's desire and my prayer to God for them is for their salvation.

2 For I testify about them that they have a zeal for God, but not according to knowledge.

3 For not knowing about the righteousness of God and seeking to establish their own, they did not subject themselves to the righteousness of God.

4 For Christ is the end of the law for righteousness to everyone who believes.

A Startling Reversal

Paul brings chapter 9 to a striking conclusion—one that exposes a deep irony rather than an unforeseen twist.

Those who were not pursuing righteousness at all obtained it.

Those who devoted themselves to pursuing righteousness failed to reach it. The issue was not effort, sincerity, or zeal.

The issue was **how righteousness was sought**.

Gentiles did not ascend toward God by obedience or achievement. God came to them. They received righteousness as a gift, through faith.

Israel, by contrast, treated the law as a ladder to climb rather than a signpost meant to lead them beyond itself. In seeking righteousness as something to be achieved rather than received, they stumbled over the very means God had provided.

Why Christ Becomes the Stumbling Stone

Romans 9:32–33

A stumbling stone is not hidden or unclear. It is encountered directly in one's path—solid, unavoidable, and decisive. The problem is not that the stone is confusing, but that it stands in the way of forward motion.

This is why Christ Himself becomes the dividing line.

He does not merely offer guidance; He stands squarely in the path of every attempt to reach God apart from Him. He offers righteousness as a gift, not a wage. He calls sinners to trust, not to perform. He requires surrender, not contribution.

For those determined to establish their own righteousness, Christ is not a help but a hindrance. He blocks every path built on human effort or moral achievement.

Paul reminds us that God placed this stone openly:

33 "Behold, I am laying in Zion a stone of stumbling and a rock of offense,

And the one who believes upon Him will not be put to shame."

The same Christ who causes some to stumble becomes a sure foundation for others. Everything turns on a single question: **Will we submit, or will we try to go around Him?**

Jesus illustrates this contrast with piercing clarity in Luke 18: 13-14

13 "But the tax collector... was beating his chest, saying, 'God, be propitious to me, the sinner!'

14 I tell you, this man went down to his house justified rather than the other..."

The tax collector asks for mercy and goes home justified.

The Pharisee is disciplined and confident, but his confidence rests in himself. His prayer never truly reaches God because it never leaves himself.

Paul is making the same point. Israel's failure was not a lack of devotion. It was a refusal to submit to God's way of saving.

Paul's Grief Beneath the Argument

Paul pauses to reveal his heart again in Romans 10:1

1 "Brothers, my heart's desire and my prayer to God for them is for their salvation."

Sovereignty has not cooled his compassion. Truth has not silenced his prayers. He longs for his people to see what they have missed.

That longing leads him directly to the truth Israel misunderstood—and the truth on which everything turns.

Zeal Without Knowledge

Paul is careful and compassionate here. In verses 2 and 3, he explains why his prayer for Israel is necessary. These verses uncover the tragic disconnect between Israel's sincerity and Israel's submission, preparing us to see why Christ alone can resolve what zeal cannot.

Paul begins by affirming what is genuinely present:
2 "For I testify about them that they have a zeal for God, but not in accordance with knowledge."

Their zeal was real. Their devotion was sincere. Paul does not question their intensity or dismiss their religious seriousness. But zeal, however earnest, cannot save when it is detached from truth. Sincerity does not equal righteousness.

Paul then names the deeper problem beneath that zeal:

3 "For not knowing about the righteousness of God and seeking to establish their own, they did not subject themselves to the righteousness of God."

This was not ignorance in the sense of never hearing the truth. It was a refusal to submit to it. Israel wanted righteousness, but on their own terms. What stood in the way was not a lack of effort, but **resistance**.

Self-righteousness is not merely moral striving; it is a posture that refuses to bow.

Christ: The End of the Law for Righteousness

4 "For Christ is the end of the law for righteousness to everyone who believes."

Paul is not saying Israel cared too much about the law. He is saying they misunderstood its purpose.

The word *end* (telos) carries two inseparable ideas: **goal** and **completion**. The law was never meant to be a rival path to salvation. It revealed God's holiness, exposed human sin, and pointed forward to the need for a greater righteousness than obedience could produce.

Christ fulfilled what the law demanded.

He bore what the law exposed.

He accomplished what the law promised.

When Paul says Christ is the end of the law for righteousness, he is not announcing a rupture in God's plan, but its fulfillment. The law was always meant to lead God's people to trust, not self-reliance.

Righteousness is no longer found by striving under the law, but by trusting the One to whom the law was always pointing.

A Gentle Landing Before Moving Forward

The tragedy Paul describes is not a lack of effort, but a misplaced trust. Israel ran hard, but past Christ.

The hope Paul proclaims is not moral reform, but faith. And the promise stands unshaken as Paul will teach as we move into Romans 10:5-21.

11 "Whoever believes upon Him will not be put to shame."

Paul will now press forward to explain how this righteousness by faith is proclaimed, heard, and believed—how God calls sinners through the gospel, and how human response unfolds within God's saving purpose.

9

Chapter 9

Not by Climbing, but by Believing

Romans 10:5-21

Up to this point, Paul has shown us who truly belongs to the people of God—those included in His saving mercy—and why.

God's mercy is sovereign. He calls whom He wills, and His purposes do not fail. But now Paul turns to the human side of the story. He begins to show how people actually receive the righteousness God provides.

Romans 10 is where the road meets the heart. It asks a searching question:

How does a sinner become right with God? And why do some receive this righteousness while others resist it?

Paul's answer is both freeing and confronting. Righteousness is not reached by effort, ascent, or spiritual climbing. It does not come through moral achievement or religious intensity.

Instead, it comes by faith. God does not ask us to climb up to heaven or descend into the depths to secure salvation. He has already come down in Christ, and He has already accomplished the work.

This chapter exposes a pattern repeated throughout history. Some strive endlessly to earn what God freely gives. Others, often the least expected, receive righteousness simply by believing. The difference is not sincerity or effort, but whether one is willing to stop climbing and trust what God has already done.

What follows is not an abstract argument, but a gracious invitation. Paul walks us through the contrast between law and faith, effort and trust, distance and nearness. And he makes one truth unmistakably clear: salvation is not found by reaching upward, but by believing what God has already brought near.

The Text

5 For Moses writes about the righteousness which is of the Law: "The man who does these things shall live by them."
6 But the righteousness of faith speaks in this way: "Do not say in your heart, 'Who will go up into heaven?' (that is, to bring Christ down),
7 or 'Who will go down into the abyss?' (that is, to bring Christ up from the dead).
8 But what does it say? "The word is near you, in your mouth and in your heart"—that is, the word of faith which we are preaching,

9 that if you confess with your mouth Jesus as Lord, and believe in your heart that God raised Him from the dead, you will be saved;

10 for with the heart a person believes, leading to righteousness, and with the mouth he confesses, leading to salvation.

11 For the Scripture says, "Whoever believes upon Him will not be put to shame."

12 For there is no distinction between Jew and Greek, for the same Lord is Lord of all, abounding in riches for all who call on Him;

13 for "Whoever calls on the name of the Lord will be saved."

14 How then will they call on Him in whom they have not believed? How will they believe in Him whom they have not heard? And how will they hear without a preacher?

15 And how will they preach unless they are sent? Just as it is written, "How beautiful are the feet of those who bring good news of good things!"

16 However, they did not all heed the good news; for Isaiah says, "Lord, who has believed our report?"

17 So faith comes from hearing, and hearing by the word of Christ.

18 But I say, surely they have never heard, have they? Indeed they have; "Their voice has gone out into all the earth, and their words to the ends of the world."

19 But I say, surely Israel did not know, did they? First Moses says, "I will make you jealous by that which is not a nation, by a nation without understanding will I anger you."

20 And Isaiah is very bold and says, "I was found by those who did not seek Me, I became manifest to those who did not ask for Me."

21 But as for Israel He says, "All the day long I have stretched

out My hands to a disobedient and obstinate people."

Righteousness Based on Law: What the Law Actually Requires

Paul begins exactly where a Jewish reader would expect him to begin—with Moses. He allows the Law to speak in its own terms, without softening or qualifying its demands.

5 "For Moses writes about the righteousness which is of the Law: 'The man who does these things shall live by them.'"

The principle Moses states is straightforward and uncompromising. If righteousness is pursued through the Law, it must be obtained by **doing** exactly what the Law commands. Life is promised on the basis of obedience—not desire, not effort, not sincerity, but performance.

The Law does not evaluate motivation.
  It does not grade on a curve.
  It does not reward intention.

The Law promises life only to the one who does all that it requires. This is why Paul carefully states precisely before it in verse 4:

"For Christ is the end of the law for righteousness to everyone who believes."

Now he explains why that statement matters so deeply. The Law never offered righteousness gradually or partially. It never functioned as a system of improvement or moral progress. It demanded full, personal, and continual obedience. To seek righteousness through the Law is to accept its terms completely.

The Law is not cruel.

It is clear.

And once its standard is understood, the conclusion is unavoidable: if righteousness depends on doing, then anyone who fails at any point stands condemned. The Law does not rescue sinners; it exposes their need. And that exposure is precisely what makes Christ not optional, but necessary.

In verses 6-7, Paul reaches back again to Moses—but this time not to law-keeping, but to grace. The righteousness of faith does not ask us to ascend or descend. It does not demand heroic effort. It rests in what God has already done.

You do not have to climb.

You do not have to descend.

God has already come down.

Christ descended from heaven. Christ rose from the dead. The work is finished. The word is near.

The Word Is Near: Faith From the Heart

Paul prepares the reader carefully before he ever speaks about confession or belief. He begins by emphasizing nearness—not

68

effort and not achievement.

8 "But what does it say? 'The word is near you, in your mouth and in your heart'—that is, the word of faith which we are preaching."

Righteousness by faith does not require a journey upward or downward. It does not demand that a sinner reach for something far away or hidden. God has already brought salvation near. His word has been spoken. The message has been preached. The truth is accessible—not because it is simple, but because God has revealed it and brought it near.

That is the setting for what follows.

9 "That if you confess with your mouth Jesus as Lord, and believe in your heart that God raised Him from the dead, you will be saved;
10 for with the heart a person believes, leading to righteousness, and with the mouth he confesses, leading to salvation."

Paul is not prescribing steps to follow or words to recite. He is describing the natural response that arises when a heart believes the words God has already spoken and placed within reach.

Faith begins in the heart. It is an inward trust—believing that God has acted in Christ by coming near to us, accomplishing what we could not, and opening the way back to Him. Jesus lived, died, and was raised so that sinners could be made right with God.

To believe is to stop relying on ourselves and to rest in Christ alone. No amount of effort, goodness, or religious activity can do what He has already done.

When that trust is real, it does not stay silent. It expresses itself verbally. A believing heart naturally speaks, not to prove anything, but because it has already found rest.

Confessing "Jesus is Lord" is not a magical phrase or a religious requirement added to faith. It is simply the outward expression of what the heart has already embraced. The mouth speaks because something has changed within.

Confession does not create new life.

It reveals it.

Paul's order matters. Belief leads to righteousness. Confession follows as its fruit. Salvation is not secured by saying the right words, but by trusting the only Savior—the One whom God has already brought near.

Salvation is not achieved by effort or spiritual climbing. It is received by faith. The righteousness God requires is the righteousness He Himself provides.

The Promise Is Open to All

Paul now widens the lens. After explaining how righteousness is received by faith, he makes clear who this promise is for.

11 "Whoever believes upon Him will not be put to shame."
12 For there is no distinction between Jew and Greek, for the same Lord is Lord of all, abounding in riches for all who call on Him;

13 for "Whoever calls on the name of the Lord will be saved."

Paul begins with reassurance. To believe in Christ is not to risk disappointment or rejection. Those who entrust themselves to Him will not be put to shame—they will not find that their hope was misplaced. Faith in Christ is never exposed as foolish in the end.

He then addresses a boundary that mattered deeply in Paul's world: the division between Jew and Gentile. For centuries, Israel had lived with clear markers of distinction—covenants, laws, promises, and identity. But Paul insists that when it comes to salvation, those distinctions no longer determine access.

There is **one Lord**, and He is Lord of all.

That means the same Christ who receives Jewish believers also receives Gentile believers. The same mercy, the same righteousness, and the same salvation are offered without preference or hierarchy. God is not restrained by ethnicity, background, moral history, or religious experience. He is "abounding in riches" toward all who call on Him.

Paul reinforces this by repeating the promise again in verse 13:
"Whoever calls on the name of the Lord will be saved."

Calling does not describe a special ritual or a certain kind of prayer. It describes dependence. To call on the Lord is to turn toward Him in trust—to appeal to Him because there is nowhere else to go. It is the language of faith expressed aloud.

This matters deeply for the uninformed reader. Paul is saying that salvation is not reserved for those who know enough, do enough, or belong to the right group. It is not earned by background or sustained by performance. It is received by faith.

The promise is intentionally broad.

Whoever believes.

Whoever calls.

The gospel does not belong to one people or one culture. Jew and Gentile stand on the same ground before the same Lord. And no one, no matter how unlikely, who comes to Christ in faith is turned away.

Why Proclamation Matters

Paul now traces the ordinary, God-appointed path by which salvation actually reaches people. If righteousness comes by faith, and faith rests on hearing, then the message itself must be spoken.

He lays this out by asking a series of connected questions, each one depending on the one before it:

14 How then will they call on Him in whom they have not believed? How will they believe in Him whom they have not heard? And how will they hear without a preacher?
15 And how will they preach unless they are sent? Just as it is written, "How beautiful are the feet of those who bring good news of good things!"

Paul's reasoning moves backward along the path of salvation.

Calling on Christ requires belief. Belief requires hearing. Hearing requires someone to speak. And speaking requires being sent. Salvation does not arrive through private insight or silent discovery. God has chosen proclamation, words spoken aloud, as the means by which faith is awakened.

To show that this has always been God's design, Paul quotes Scripture.

Isaiah 52:7
7 How beautiful on the mountains are the feet of him who brings good news,
Who announces peace
And brings good news of good things,
Who announces salvation,
And says to Zion, "Your God reigns!"

In Isaiah's day, the "beautiful feet" belonged to a messenger announcing deliverance and the reign of God to a people longing for salvation. The beauty was not in the messenger himself, but in the message he carried—news of peace, restoration, and God's saving rule.

In Romans 10:15, Paul deliberately applies that same image to the proclamation of the gospel. The message has reached its fulfillment in Christ, but the method has not changed. God still sends messengers. Salvation still comes through words spoken and heard.

Those who carry the message of salvation, ordinary people speaking extraordinary news, are called "beautiful," not because of who they are, but because of what they bring. They announce peace with God, forgiveness of sins, and reconciliation through Christ.

The gospel spreads because it is spoken.

Faith grows because the Word is heard.

And salvation reaches sinners because God sends messengers.

This is why Paul can say with confidence:

Sovereignty does not silence mission. It gives it confidence.

God saves through the Word He sends, spoken by people He appoints, to hearts He opens.

Israel's Responsibility in Rejection

At this point, Paul addresses a necessary and unavoidable question:

If Israel has not believed, is it because they never truly heard? Paul's answer is direct and unmistakable. **They did hear.** He begins by acknowledging the painful reality of Israel's response:

16 However, they did not all heed the good news; for Isaiah says,

"Lord, who has believed our report?"

The problem was not the absence of a message, but the refusal to receive it. The good news was announced, proclaimed, and made known—but it was not obeyed. Hearing occurred. Belief did not.

Paul then draws a clear conclusion about how faith normally arises:

17 So faith comes from hearing, and hearing by the word of Christ.

Faith is not self-generated. It is awakened by God's Word. And since faith depends on hearing, Paul anticipates the next objection: perhaps Israel never truly heard that Word. He answers that objection immediately.

18 But I say, surely they have never heard, have they? Indeed they have;
   "Their voice has gone out into all the earth,
   And their words to the ends of the world."

In verse 18, Paul has just quoted Psalm 19:4—*"Their voice has gone out into all the earth, and their words to the ends of the world"*—a psalm that originally describes how creation itself declares the glory of God everywhere. Paul borrows that language intentionally, not to suggest that creation saves, but to emphasize reach. Just as the testimony of creation is not hidden, localized, or inaccessible, so the message God sent concerning Christ was not confined or withheld. The Word had gone out. The message had been spoken. Israel was not isolated from hearing it. The problem was not silence, but response. God had spoken, and His testimony had reached them.

The Word had gone out. The message had been proclaimed. Israel was not cut off from hearing it. The problem was not silence, but response. God had spoken, and His testimony had reached them.

Still, Paul presses further and removes the final possible excuse. If Israel heard the message and if the message was clear, then one question remains: Did Israel truly understand what God was doing? To answer that, Paul reaches back to Israel's own foundation—to Moses himself, whose words Israel could not dismiss.

Moses Foretells Israel's Jealousy

19 But I say, surely Israel did not know, did they? First Moses says,

"I will make you jealous by that which is not a nation,
By a nation without understanding will I anger you."

Paul's point is decisive. Israel's failure cannot be explained by lack of knowledge. Long before Christ came, Moses himself warned that God would provoke Israel to jealousy by showing mercy to outsiders. The inclusion of the Gentiles was not an afterthought or a late correction. It was embedded in Israel's own Scriptures from the beginning.

God had already said that He would use those outside the covenant nation to expose Israel's resistance and awaken her conscience.

Paul does not stop with Moses. To make his point unmistakable, he turns to Isaiah—whose words speak with even greater clarity and force.

20 And Isaiah is very bold and says,

"I was found by those who did not seek Me,
I became manifest to those who did not ask for Me."

Isaiah originally spoke these words to describe God's sovereign initiative toward those outside Israel. Paul applies them directly to the Gentiles. They were not raised under the Law. They were not pursuing covenant righteousness. They were not seeking God on their own terms. Yet God revealed Himself to them.

They did not find God because they were better seekers. They found Him because He made Himself known.

Paul's final quotation deepens the contrast even further. After showing God's initiative toward those who were not seeking Him, Paul turns back to Israel—not to accuse, but to reveal God's posture toward her.

21 But as for Israel he says,
"All the day long I have stretched out My hands
To a disobedient and obstinate people."

Paul is not inventing this image. He is drawing directly from Isaiah's words:

Isaiah 65:2
2"I have spread out My hands all day long to a rebellious people,
Who walk in the way which is not good, following their own thoughts."

Isaiah shows that this posture is not new. God's stance toward Israel has long been one of patient, outstretched appeal—even in the face of resistance. He is not distant, silent, or indifferent. He is pictured inviting, calling, and enduring refusal.

Israel's rejection is not explained by divine absence, but by persistent resistance.

Paul does not resolve Israel's future here—that work belongs ahead in Romans 11. For now, he establishes what cannot be avoided:

God spoke.
God sent messengers.
God revealed Himself.
God invited.

Israel heard.
Israel knew.
Israel resisted.

Rejection was real. Responsibility remains.

Paul allows the weight to settle here. God is sovereign. People are responsible. Scripture refuses to flatten either truth. God's purposes stand, and human response matters.

Drawing It Together

Righteousness does not come by striving, but by believing.
It is not gained by climbing, but by trusting.
It does not rest on human merit, but on Christ's finished work.
And it spreads not through silence, but through proclama-

tion.

The invitation still stands:
   "Whoever believes upon Him will not be put to shame."

Romans 10:5–21 brings Paul's argument to a clear point of responsibility.

This chapter explains why Israel is accountable for unbelief and how righteousness is received—not by striving, but by faith that comes through hearing the proclaimed gospel. God has spoken, Christ has been made known, and the call to believe has gone out.

Romans 11 will build on these truths, showing how Israel's present unbelief fits within God's larger purposes—unbelief that is real and accountable, yet neither total nor final. In doing so, it will also deepen our understanding of God's calling itself: how He remains faithful to His promises, how mercy operates over time, and how those whom God calls are gathered, sustained, and kept—not by human strength, but by His steadfast grace.

Chapter 10

When Blessings Become Curses

Romans 11:1–10

Millions of people suffer from a medical condition known as sclerosis—the gradual hardening of arteries, tissues, and organs that restrict life and slowly damage what was meant to function freely. The effects can be subtle at first, but over time they become severe and even fatal.

In Romans 11, Paul brings us face to face with a spiritual condition that is just as real and far more serious: the hardening of the heart.

This is not sudden rebellion or loud rejection of God. It is a gradual spiritual sclerosis. Eyes grow dull. Ears grow unresponsive. Familiar truths no longer stir the soul. Over time, the heart becomes resistant to the very grace it has encountered. Unless God intervenes, this condition leads not merely to spiritual weakness, but to spiritual death.

For physical sclerosis, there is often no cure. But for sclerosis of the heart, Scripture holds out real hope. There is a remedy, and Christ Himself has provided it through the gospel.

Before Paul explains that remedy, however, he asks us to face a doctrine that is difficult to hear and difficult to teach—yet given to us in Scripture for our warning and our good: **the doctrine of judicial hardening.** Some hearts are confirmed in the direction they have chosen. Some are passed over—not arbitrarily, but in righteous judgment.

God's warnings are not signs of harshness. They are acts of mercy.

And Paul will not allow us to keep this doctrine at a safe distance. He is not addressing the openly irreligious outsider, but moral, devout, Scripture-aware people—people who enjoy spiritual privilege, know the language of faith, and live surrounded by religious blessing.

For such people, the danger is especially real.

When spiritual privileges are not united with faith in Christ, those very blessings can become sources of hardness rather than life.

With that sober reality in view, Paul explains what has happened to Israel in the present age, why some have received the righteousness they longed for by trusting God's mercy, while others—seeking the same blessing—missed it by refusing God's way.

The Text

1 I say then, has God rejected His people? May it never be! For I too am an Israelite, a seed of Abraham, of the tribe of Benjamin.

2 God has not rejected His people whom He foreknew. Or do you not know what the Scripture says in the passage about Elijah, how he appeals to God against Israel?

3 "Lord, they have killed Your prophets, they have torn down Your altars, and I alone am left, and they are seeking my life."

4 But what does the divine response say to him? "I have left for Myself seven thousand men who have not bowed the knee to Baal."

5 In this way then, at the present time, a remnant according to God's gracious choice has also come to be.

6 But if it is by grace, it is no longer of works, otherwise grace is no longer grace.

7 What then? What Israel is seeking, it has not obtained, but the chosen obtained it, and the rest were hardened;

8 just as it is written,

"God gave them a spirit of stupor,

Eyes to see not and ears to hear not,

Down to this very day."

9 And David says,

"Let their table become a snare and a trap,

And a stumbling block and a retribution to them.

10 Let their eyes be darkened to see not,

And bend their backs forever."

Setting the Context: Israel's Partial and Temporary Rejection

Before Paul speaks of hardening, he deliberately sets boundaries around how it must be understood. Romans 11 is not an announcement that God has abandoned Israel. It is a careful explanation of how Israel's present condition fits within God's ongoing faithfulness.

Paul raises the question himself so no misunderstanding can take root:

1 "I say then, has God rejected His people? May it never be!"

That emphatic denial establishes the framework for everything that follows. What Paul is about to explain must be read within this assurance.

To support his claim, Paul points not only to doctrine, but to history—and to a moment when God's people appeared nearly extinguished.

3 "Lord, they have killed Your prophets, they have torn down Your altars, and I alone am left, and they are seeking my life."
4 But what does the divine response say to him?
"I have left for Myself seven thousand men who have not bowed the knee to Baal."

Paul is recalling Elijah's despair. From Elijah's vantage point, Israel's faithfulness appeared to have vanished entirely. The nation seemed apostate. True worship seemed extinct. Elijah believed he was the last remaining servant of the Lord. But

Elijah's perception was not God's reality.

God had quietly preserved a faithful remnant—unknown to Elijah, unseen by the nation, but fully known and sustained by God Himself. Their faithfulness did not depend on visibility, influence, or numbers. It rested on God's preserving mercy. Paul draws the conclusion explicitly:

5 "So too at the present time there is a remnant according to God's gracious choice."

This example establishes the first guiding truth for Romans 11: Israel's rejection is partial, not total. Even in seasons of widespread unbelief, God has never been without a people. Paul makes clear that this remnant exists by grace, not by works and according to God's gracious choice.

6 "But if it is by grace, it is no longer on the basis of works; otherwise grace is no longer grace."

Israel's continued existence before God has always rested on mercy, not merit.

As the chapter unfolds, Paul will add a second guiding truth in verse 25: Israel's present condition is also temporary, not final.

With the first truth firmly established—and the second held in view—Paul moves forward to speak about hardening. What follows is not a declaration of abandonment, but an explanation of how judgment and mercy are operating together within God's redemptive plan.

A Necessary Clarification

Having established that Israel's rejection is partial, not total—
and that it rests on grace rather than works—Paul now clarifies
what that actually looks like in lived reality. The question is
no longer *whether* God has failed His people, but *how* God's
purposes are presently unfolding within Israel itself.

Up to this point, Paul has spoken in broad categories: remnant, grace, rejection. Now he names the results plainly. Not
to speculate, and not to accuse, but to help the church see
clearly what is happening, and why it does not contradict God's
faithfulness.

What Paul describes next is not three different peoples, but
three outcomes experienced within the same nation at the same
time.

Three Outcomes Within Israel

Paul now summarizes Israel's present condition with careful
precision.

I. Israel as a Whole Sought Righteousness and Did Not
Obtain It

Israel's failure was not indifference. These were moral,

religious, Scripture-loving people. Their problem was not zeal, but direction. They pursued righteousness through performance rather than faith. What they sought was good. How they sought it was fatal.

As Paul has already explained:

Romans 10:2–3
2 For I testify about them that they have a zeal for God, but not according to knowledge.
3 For not knowing about the righteousness of God and seeking to establish their own, they did not subject themselves to the righteousness of God.

II. The Elect Within Israel Obtained Righteousness by Grace

Within the nation, God preserved a remnant. Those who believed did so only because God intervened by grace. Salvation leaves no room for boasting and gives all glory to God.

Romans 11:5–6
5 "…a remnant according to God's gracious choice…
6 But if it is by grace, it is no longer of works."

III. The Rest Were Hardened

Paul then states the sobering reality in verse 7: "The rest were hardened."

The verb *were hardened* is passive. Paul is not describing people suddenly becoming unbelieving, nor is he suggesting that God creates unbelief in the heart. He is describing **judicial**

hardening—God confirming people in the path they have persistently chosen. When truth is resisted long enough, God may hand a person over to that resistance rather than restrain it.

What Judicial Hardening Looks Like

Before Paul explains *why* some are hardened, he helps us understand *what* that hardening looks like in lived experience. He is not describing sudden rebellion or open hostility toward God. What he describes is far more subtle—and therefore far more dangerous.

Paul reaches back into Israel's Scriptures to show that this condition has appeared before, and that God Himself has warned about it.

8 "God gave them a spirit of stupor,
   Eyes to see not and ears to hear not,
   Down to this very day."

This language comes from both Deuteronomy and Isaiah. It describes a kind of spiritual numbness. Truth is present, but it no longer penetrates. Words are heard, but they no longer register. Scripture is read, sermons are listened to, religious life continues—but the heart is no longer responding.

Paul emphasizes the seriousness of this condition by adding, *"down to this very day."* This is not momentary confusion or a passing season of doubt. It is a settled state that can persist over time.

Isaiah paints this condition with vivid clarity:

Isaiah 29:9–11

9 Astonish yourselves and be astonished,
   Blind yourselves and be blind;
   They become drunk, but not with wine;
   They stagger, but not with strong drink.
10 For Yahweh has poured over you a spirit of deep sleep;
   He has shut your eyes, the prophets;
   And He has covered your heads, the seers.
11 The entire vision will be to you like the words of a sealed
book, which when they give it to the one who is literate, saying,
"Please read this," he will say, "I cannot, for it is sealed.

The problem Isaiah describes is not the absence of revelation.
The book is there. The words exist. But understanding is
withheld. Truth stands openly before them, yet it does not take
hold. Words are heard, but they no longer awaken the heart
and penetrate the soul.

Jesus Himself describes this same pattern during His ministry.
When truth is persistently resisted, further light is not always
granted.

Matthew 13:14–15

13 Therefore I speak to them in parables; because while seeing
they do not see, and while hearing they do not hear, nor do
they understand.
14 And in them the prophecy of Isaiah is being fulfilled, which
says,

You will keep on hearing, but will not understand;
You will keep on seeing, but will not perceive;
15 For the heart of this people has become dull,
And with their ears they scarcely hear,
And they have closed their eyes,
Lest they would see with their eyes,
Hear with their ears,
And understand with their heart and return,
And I would heal them.'

Notice the progression. What begins as resistance becomes incapacity. John later shows this pattern reaching its most sobering point in Israel's response to Christ:

John 12:37–30
37 But though He had done so many signs before them, they *still* were not believing in Him,
38 so that the word of Isaiah the prophet might be fulfilled, which he spoke: "Lord, who has believed our report? And to whom has the arm of the Lord been revealed?"
39 For this reason they could not believe, for Isaiah said again,
30 "He has blinded their eyes and He hardened their heart, lest they see with their eyes and understand with their heart, and return and I heal them."

First, they *would not* believe. Then, they *could not*. Persistent refusal gives way to inability. This is judicial hardening—not arbitrary cruelty, but righteous confirmation. God does not force unbelief; He may, in judgment, cease restraining it.

Paul includes this doctrine not to provoke fear or speculation, but to awaken sobriety. Grace resisted does not remain neutral.

Light refused can become light withdrawn.

And yet even here, Paul is not finished speaking. Hardening, as he will soon explain, is neither the whole story nor the final word.

When Blessings Become Traps

Paul now describes one of the most sobering realities in Scripture—not how God withholds good things, but how good things themselves become dangerous when they are trusted in the wrong way. To make his point, Paul reaches back to David's own words quoted from Psalm 69:22:

22 May their table before them become a snare;

And when they are in peace, *may it become* a trap.

The image is striking. A table is meant for nourishment, rest, and fellowship. It is a place of provision and blessing. Yet Paul says that this very table can become a snare.

The danger is not in the blessing itself, but in what the heart does with it.

Israel's privileges were real and significant. They had the Law, the temple, the sacrifices, the covenants, and the promises. These were not empty symbols; they were genuine gifts from God. But when those gifts were trusted apart from Christ—when they became substitutes rather than signposts—they no longer led to life. They became obstacles.

God had warned of this long before in Malachi 2:2: *"I will curse your blessings..."*

Blessings are meant to lead us to God, not replace Him. When spiritual privileges become objects of confidence instead of means of grace, they do not soften the heart—they harden it.

Paul's warning is not meant to terrify, but to awaken. Good gifts, even sacred ones, cannot save. Only Christ can. And when anything—even God's own blessings—is trusted in His place, what was meant for life can quietly become a trap.

Darkness and Bondage

10 "Let their eyes be darkened to see not,
 And bend their backs forever."

Paul is still drawing from David's words, and the imagery deepens. What began as resistance has now become condition. Eyes that once could see are darkened. Backs that once stood upright are bent low.

This is not merely intellectual blindness. It is a life increasingly weighed down. The picture is of people laboring under a burden they were never meant to carry—striving to establish righteousness on their own, bearing the weight of law-keeping, self-reliance, and unrelenting effort—while grace remains near, offered but refused.

The tragedy is not that God demands too much. It is that people insist on carrying what God never asked them to bear. When righteousness is pursued apart from Christ, the soul does not rise; it stoops. What was meant to lead to life becomes a lifelong burden.

Paul is not describing sudden punishment, but settled conse-
quence. Darkness deepens. The posture hardens. What begins
as refusal becomes bondage.

And yet even here, Paul is explaining—not delighting in
judgment, but helping us see where persistent resistance leads
when mercy is continually set aside.

Holding Judgment and Mercy Together

Paul has not taken us this far to provoke fear or curiosity, but
to guard us from a dangerous misunderstanding—that God is
unjust in the way He saves. What Romans 11 has shown so far
is not a God who delights in hardening, but a God who acts
righteously toward sinners and mercifully toward those He
saves.

Grace, by definition, is undeserved. Those who receive it
have no ground for boasting. And judgment, by definition, is
just. Those who remain in unbelief are not treated unfairly; they
are left where persistent resistance leads. Paul is not inviting us
to speculate about why God saves one person and not another.
He is teaching us to see sin clearly, mercy rightly, and God
rightly.

But Paul is not finished.

If everything stopped here, we might wrongly conclude that
hardening is the final word. It is not. Paul will now turn our
attention to something equally true and equally necessary: how
God is using Israel's stumbling to bring mercy to the world—
and how that same mercy will yet return to Israel in a way that
magnifies grace even further.

Romans 11:11–16 shifts the focus from judgment to purpose, from stumbling to salvation, from loss to unexpected gain. What looks like an ending is not the end. What appears to be rejection is not abandonment. God's redemptive plan is still unfolding—and it is far more generous than it first appears.

11

Chapter 11

Riches for the Nations

Romans 11:11–16

Before Paul moves forward, he gathers the argument he has been carefully building. In Romans 9, he addressed Israel's past election. In Romans 10, he confronted Israel's present condition: widespread unbelief and real responsibility. Now, in Romans 11, Paul turns the reader's attention toward Israel's future. He is no longer asking only what has happened, but where God's redemptive purpose is moving.

Paul speaks here with historical clarity, tracing the unfolding pattern of God's work from the first coming of Christ through the present age. At the same time, he speaks with prophetic steadiness, showing that God's mercy toward the Gentiles is not the final chapter of the story. Later in the chapter, he will name part of this plan a mystery, and he will explain that Israel's hardening lasts only until the fullness of the Gentiles has come in. God's mercy toward the nations is real and expansive, but it does not cancel His future mercy toward Israel.

Paul is also attentive to the life of the church itself. The Roman congregation lived within real tension. Jewish and Gentile believers were tempted toward suspicion, pride, and division. Paul does not address those tensions indirectly. He applies the gospel as a remedy, shaping how Gentile believers are to understand their place in God's plan and how they are to hold space for God's future mercy toward Israel. He wants The Church to see that Israel's story and The Church's story are bound together, and that blessing for the nations is inseparable from God's faithfulness to His ancient promises.

The Text

11 I say then, did they not stumble so as to fall? May it never be! But by their transgression salvation has come to the Gentiles, to make them jealous.

12 Now if their transgression is riches for the world and their failure is riches for the Gentiles, how much more will their fullness be!

13 But I am speaking to you who are Gentiles. Inasmuch then as I am an apostle of Gentiles, I magnify my ministry

14 if somehow I might move to jealousy my fellow countrymen and save some of them.

15 For if their rejection is the reconciliation of the world, what will their acceptance be but life from the dead?

16 And if the first piece of dough is holy, the lump is also; and if the root is holy, the branches are too.

In verses 11–16, Paul traces a single movement with several layers. He begins with Israel's present stumbling, shows how that stumble opened the door of mercy to the nations, and then lifts the reader's eyes toward a future restoration that surpasses the present moment. What unfolds is not a series of disconnected ideas, but one unfolding purpose—moving from loss to mercy, and from mercy to hope.

Paul begins by naming Israel's present condition with honesty and care.

11 "I say then, did they not stumble so as to fall? May it never be! But by their transgression salvation has come to the Gentiles, to make them jealous."

Israel has stumbled, but Paul is careful with his words. A stumble is real and serious, but it is not the same as a final fall. Israel's rejection of her Messiah was not indifference. These were Scripture-loving, morally serious, deeply religious people. Their failure was not a lack of zeal, but a misdirected pursuit. They sought righteousness through performance rather than faith and stumbled over the very stone God placed openly before them.

Yet Paul insists that even this tragic stumble was not outside God's redemptive purpose.

Israel's transgression became the means by which salvation flowed outward to the Gentiles. What Israel rejected, the nations received. Again and again in the book of Acts, this pattern appears. When the gospel was proclaimed and met with hardened resistance among many in Israel, it did not stall. It moved outward. Gentiles heard, believed, and rejoiced as the word of salvation reached them.

Israel's rejection was real. It was a genuine loss. But Paul shows that God did not waste it. Mercy overflowed beyond Israel's borders, and the world was enriched.

Paul then presses further, revealing that this outward movement of mercy was never meant to end with the Gentiles.

11, 14 "...salvation has come to the Gentiles, to make them jealous... if somehow I might move to jealousy my fellow countrymen and save some of them."

God's mercy toward the nations carries a secondary aim. It is meant to provoke Israel, not to petty envy, but to holy longing. As Gentiles come to know the God of Israel through Israel's Messiah, Israel is meant to see what she has missed. Paul himself embodies this purpose. He magnifies his ministry among the Gentiles not to distance himself from his people, but in hope that some of his own might be drawn back and saved.

Gentiles benefit from Israel's unbelief, but never in a way that invites pride. Their inclusion is not a reward for insight or effort. It is mercy. And that mercy is meant to shine so clearly that it awakens desire rather than resentment.

Paul is not encouraging Gentile believers toward pride or self-importance. He is showing that genuine life in Christ—marked by humility, worship, and nearness to God—becomes a living testimony to the emptiness of religion without the Messiah.

From there, Paul lifts the reader's eyes beyond the present moment altogether.

12 "Now if their transgression is riches for the world and their failure is riches for the Gentiles, how much more will their fullness be!

15 For if their rejection is the reconciliation of the world, what will their acceptance be but life from the dead?"

Paul argues from lesser to greater. If Israel's loss brought blessing to the nations, what will Israel's restoration bring? The present age, marked by Gentile inclusion, is rich with mercy. But it is not the climax of the story.

The phrase *life from the dead* is deliberately arresting. Paul is not describing mere improvement or reform. He is pointing toward resurrection life, the fullness of new covenant blessing brought to completion. Later in the chapter, Paul will speak plainly: Israel's hardening lasts only until the fullness of the Gentiles comes in, and then Israel is brought to salvation.

The prophets spoke of this future with remarkable consistency. They described a time of restoration, renewal, cleansing, and peace under the reign of the Messiah. This hope is not peripheral to Paul's argument. It is the horizon toward which he is moving.

Israel's restoration is not a side story. It is bound up with the glory of Christ's reign and the final blessing of the whole people of God.

Paul closes this section by shaping how Gentile believers are to understand the present moment:

- Israel's stumbling is not final.
- Gentile mercy is real—but never grounds for pride.
- The future of God's people is shared, not divided.

Paul is shaping how both Jews and Gentiles are meant to understand the present stage of God's redemptive plan. Romans 11:11–16 is not given to invite speculation, but to form understanding. Paul steadies the church's confidence in God's faithfulness and guards it from arrogance. God's plan is moving patiently and purposefully toward a future in which His mercy will be seen as wiser, fuller, and more far-reaching than it first appeared.

Here, Paul pauses. Israel has stumbled, but not beyond recovery. Gentiles have received mercy, but not as an end in itself. And God's promises continue to move toward their fulfillment, held together by the same faithful mercy that has carried the story from the beginning.

12

Chapter 12

Our Spiritual Heritage

Romans 11:17–24

Paul has already traced the broad contours of God's saving plan. Israel's stumbling has not meant Israel's ruin. Their rejection has opened the door to the nations. And yet God has not abandoned His ancient promises.

Now Paul slows the reader down. He does not introduce a new argument, but presses what he has already explained into the life of The Church itself.

The problem he addresses is not doctrinal confusion alone. It is posture.

Grace, once received, can quietly turn into entitlement. And when it does, unity fractures. So Paul introduces an image designed to humble everyone at once.

The Text

17 But if some of the branches were broken off, and you, being a wild olive, were grafted in among them and became a partaker with them of the rich root of the olive tree,

18 do not boast against the branches; but if you do boast, remember that it is not you who supports the root, but the root supports you.

19 You will say then, "Branches were broken off so that I might be grafted in."

20 Quite right. They were broken off for their unbelief, but you stand by your faith. Do not become proud, but fear.

21 For if God did not spare the natural branches, He will not spare you either.

22 See then the kindness and severity of God: severity toward those who fell, but kindness toward you, if you continue in His kindness; otherwise you also will be cut off.

23 And they also, if they do not continue in their unbelief, will be grafted in, for God is able to graft them in again.

24 For if you were cut off from what is by nature a wild olive tree and were grafted contrary to nature into a cultivated olive tree, how much more will these, who are the natural branches, be grafted into their own olive tree?

Paul has explained the plan. Now he illustrates it in a way meant to settle into the heart.

The Olive Tree

Paul now turns to an image that gathers everything he has been saying and presses it home personally—a deliberately simple and humbling metaphor: the olive tree.

A root > A tree > Natural branches > Wild branches > Branches broken off > Branches grafted in

The Root: A Shared Inheritance

Paul has already introduced the image of the root earlier in verse 16, *"And if the first piece of dough is holy, the lump is also; and if the root is holy, the branches are too."*, and in verse 18 he makes its meaning unmistakably clear as he addresses Gentile believers directly:

18 "Do not boast against the branches; but if you do boast, remember that it is not you who support the root, but the root supports you."

That single sentence establishes the direction of everything that follows. Life does not flow upward from the branches. It flows outward from the root. Whatever God set apart at the beginning determines what can live from it afterward. Alongside Paul's earlier image of firstfruits, the point is the same: the beginning governs the whole.

There is a warning to the Gentiles built directly into the image itself. If the root supports the branches, then no branch—natural or grafted—stands on its own. There is no room for boasting, because there is no room for self-support.

The root represents the patriarchs and the covenant promises God made to them. The logic of the illustration requires this. The root must be more foundational than the branches it sustains. It existed before them, and it gives life to them. The branches—whether natural or grafted—do not redefine the root. They live because of it.

Later in the chapter, Paul will say that Israel remains beloved for the sake of the fathers, and that the gifts and the purposes of God are irrevocable. The story does not begin with The Church. It begins with promises God made long before any of us knew His name, and long before any of us had standing to claim them.

For Gentile believers, this is quietly displacing in the best possible way. Faith in Christ is not a new religion detached from history. It is an inclusion into an older story, one we did not originate, do not manage, and cannot reshape. Salvation is not ownership. It is participation.

The Tree: One Redeemed People

Paul introduces the full olive tree image and places both Jewish and Gentile believers inside it. Some of the original branches were broken off, and Gentile believers—described as wild olive shoots—were grafted in among those who remained. The result is not two trees standing side by side, but **one living tree**.

17 But if some of the branches were broken off, and you, being a wild olive, were grafted in among them and became a partaker with them of the rich root of the olive tree,

The tree represents the people of God as a single, continuous story across time. It is not rebuilt from scratch, and it does not change its root. Life flows from the same covenant promises God made long ago, and every branch—whether natural or grafted in—lives only by sharing in that root.

This image leaves no room for rival plans or parallel peoples of God. Israel and The Church are not separate trunks with separate futures. There is one cultivated tree, sustained by God's promises, into which believers are joined by mercy.

This clarity matters, because this passage is sometimes read as if The Church replaces Israel. Paul's illustration does not allow that conclusion. The branches that were broken off are unbelieving Jews—not Israel as a whole. And the branches that were grafted in are believing Gentiles—not Gentiles by nature. Belief, not ethnicity, explains the difference.

Paul is not describing replacement. He is describing continuity with distinction—one people sustained by grace, with room for both natural branches restored and wild branches included.

Union, not rivalry, is the point. And mercy, not merit, is the only reason any branch remains.

Wild Branches: Grace Contrary to Nature

Paul turns directly to Gentile believers and describes them as branches taken from a wild olive tree and grafted into a cultivated one. He emphasizes how unexpected—and undeserved—this is. In verse 24, he states it plainly:

24 "For if you were cut off from what is by nature a wild olive tree and were grafted contrary to nature into a cultivated olive tree, how much more will these, who are the natural branches, be grafted into their own olive tree?"

Paul is intentionally pressing the contrast. Gentiles did not belong to the cultivated tree by origin, history, or covenant promise. They were outsiders, without the Law, without the covenants, without ancestral claim. And yet God grafted them in. He brought them near. He made them partakers of the rich root.

This grafting, Paul says, is *contrary to nature*. In ordinary agriculture, wild branches do not strengthen a cultivated tree. Paul knows this. He is not giving a lesson in farming, but in grace. What has happened to the Gentiles cannot be explained by custom, worth, or advantage. It is mercy, freely given.

That is why the final clause matters so much: *"how much more will these, who are the natural branches, be grafted into their own olive tree?"*

Paul is arguing from the greater to the lesser. If God has already done the more surprising thing—grafting outsiders with no covenant claim into a cultivated tree—then the restoration of the natural branches is not only possible, but fitting. It does not require a new plan, a new people, or a new promise. It requires only the removal of unbelief.

Paul is not saying that Israel deserves restoration. He is saying that restoration remains consistent with God's faithfulness. The same mercy that acted *against nature* to bring Gentiles in is fully able to act *according to promise* to bring Israel back.

Gentile believers are not invited to assume permanence by position, but to remain dependent by faith. Their inclusion is not a reason for confidence in themselves, but for reverent gratitude toward the God who grafts, sustains, and gives life.

Paul's hope here is neither speculative nor sentimental. It rests on what God has already demonstrated. If mercy has reached this far outward, then it has not yet reached its limit.

The structure of God's redemptive work has not changed. The root still supplies life to the tree, and God remains able to graft in again those who were removed.

Pride Exposed: Unbelief and Faith

Paul anticipates a quiet but dangerous conclusion that Gentile believers might draw from Israel's unbelief.

19 "Branches were broken off so that I might be grafted in."

Paul agrees that this statement is *factually true*.

20 "Quite right."

But then he slows the reader down, because *why* the branches were broken off matters just as much as *that* they were broken off.

21 "They were broken off for unbelief, but you stand by faith."

This distinction is crucial. Israel was not removed so that Gentiles could feel superior. Branches were broken off because of **unbelief**, not because Gentiles were wiser, humbler, or more deserving. And Gentiles stand only by **faith**, not by insight, effort, or status.

Paul's warning is subtle but serious: If unbelief led to removal, then faith must never be treated as something secure by default or assumed by position. Faith is not a badge of arrival. It is a posture of dependence.

Gentile believers are not being told to fear losing salvation. Paul has already made clear in Romans 8 that nothing can separate God's people from His love in Christ. What Paul confronts here is presumption — the quiet confidence that rests on being "in" rather than on continuing trust in Christ.

The danger is not faith failing, but faith being replaced with entitlement.

If God did not spare the natural branches when unbelief hardened, then no one should treat grace as something owned, managed, or deserved. Grace does not eliminate humility; it produces it.

Faith does not say, "I belong here." Faith says, "I am here only because God has been merciful." That posture leaves no room for pride — only gratitude, vigilance, and trust.

Kindness and Severity Held Together

Paul calls the reader to look steadily at both sides of God's character.

22 "See then the kindness and severity of God."

God's kindness is seen in the grafting itself. Wild branches are brought near. Gentiles, who had no covenant claim, are made partakers of the rich root. Grace initiates. It reaches outward. It gives what was never owed.

God's severity appears where unbelief persists. Judgment is not arbitrary. It is the settled response of holiness to resistance. God is patient, but patience is not indifference.

Paul is not asking us to choose between these. He is showing that mercy, rightly understood, includes both. Severity does not contradict kindness; it clarifies it. And kindness, because it is undeserved, never becomes entitlement.

Grace does not produce casualness. It produces reverence.

Hope: God Able to Graft Again

Paul does not leave the reader with warning alone. He deliberately opens the door of hope.

23 "And they also, if they do not continue in their unbelief, will be grafted in, for God is able to graft them in again."

Israel's present condition is not God's final word. Unbelief, while real and serious, is not irreversible. Where unbelief ends, restoration remains possible, not because of Israel's ability to return, but because of God's ability to act.

Paul's confidence here is not sentimental or speculative. It rests on what God has already done. That is why Paul immediately strengthens the promise with an argument from greater to lesser:

24 "For if you were cut off from what is by nature a wild olive tree and were grafted contrary to nature into a cultivated olive tree, how much more will these, who are the natural branches, be grafted into their own olive tree?"

If God has already done the unexpected—grafting outsiders into a cultivated tree—then restoring the natural branches is not a stretch of mercy. It is well within His purpose and power.

Paul's hope is therefore reverent, not triumphal. The same mercy that reached outward to the Gentiles has not exhausted itself. It remains able to bring Israel home.

The image ends where it began—not with human certainty, but with divine capability. God is able. And that ability holds the future open.

One Landing

Paul leaves the image where it belongs—not as a weapon to wield, but as a place to rest. You do not support the root; the root supports you. Grace has come where it was not deserved.

Life flows from a source we did not create and cannot control. Faith itself is sustained by mercy, not managed by effort. And that is where Paul allows the picture to stand.

Chapter 13

A Revealed Mystery, Not a Finished Story

Romans 11:25–27

Having placed the church inside the olive tree—dependent on a root it does not support—Paul now speaks plainly. He does so not to conclude his argument, but to prevent it from being misunderstood.

What follows is not a closing statement, but a stabilizing one. Paul reveals something God had kept hidden until this moment, not to satisfy curiosity, but to guard the church from pride and from reading the present moment incorrectly.

The Text

Romans 11:25–27

25 For I do not want you, brothers, to be uninformed of this mystery, so that you will not be wise in your own estimation, that a partial hardening has happened to Israel until the fullness of the Gentiles has come in;
26 and so all Israel will be saved; just as it is written,
  "The Deliverer will come from Zion,
  He will remove ungodliness from Jacob."
27 "This is My covenant with them,
  When I take away their sins."

A Mystery Now Made Known

When Paul uses the word *mystery* in verse 25, he is not referring to something unknowable or speculative. In Paul's letters, a mystery is a truth once hidden in God's purposes but now revealed at the proper time. It is disclosed, not discovered.

Paul explicitly tells us *why* he is revealing it: so that you will not be wise in your own estimation. His concern is pastoral before it is theological. Misunderstanding God's plan here almost always produces arrogance—especially among Gentile believers who might conclude that Israel's story is finished or irrelevant.

So Paul speaks plainly.

In verse 25, he states the first element of the mystery: *a partial*

112

hardening has happened to Israel. This hardening is real, but it is qualified in two critical ways Paul has already established earlier in the chapter:

- It is partial, not total (Romans 11:5, 7).
- It is temporary, not permanent (Romans 11:11–12, 23).

Paul places this hardening under a clear boundary: until the fullness of the Gentiles has come in. History is not drifting. It is moving toward a God-appointed completion.

The Fullness of The Gentiles

When Paul speaks of *the fullness of the Gentiles* in verse 25, he is not describing a general openness to the gospel or a vague global success. He is pointing to a **definite completion**—a moment determined by God Himself.

The word *fullness* refers to a number brought to completion. God is not reacting to history as it unfolds; He is carrying out a purpose formed before it began. From among the nations, God is gathering **the full number He intends to save**, not one more and not one less. When that purpose reaches its completion, the present phase of redemptive history gives way to what follows.

This does not mean Gentiles are saved by a different plan or under a separate promise. Paul has already been clear: Gentiles are grafted into Israel's olive tree, not planted beside it (Romans 11:17–18). They share in the same root, the same covenant mercy, and the same Messiah. Their salvation rests on God's sovereign grace in Christ, just as Israel's always has.

Israel's partial hardening and Gentile inclusion are not competing explanations. Both unfold together under God's sovereign purpose, each serving a larger design He is patiently accomplishing.

Here, Paul invites us to see history through God's lens. Salvation is not random. It is not driven by human momentum or cultural shifts. God is not hoping enough will respond. He is **faithfully calling His people**, across nations and generations, according to His gracious will.

Gentile salvation, then, is not the end of the story. It is part of the story's forward movement. When the fullness God has appointed is complete, He will act again—just as surely, just as sovereignly—as He has all along.

And So All Israel Will Be Saved

With careful restraint, Paul moves to another weighty statement: and so all Israel will be saved.

Here Paul does not redefine Israel or shift his meaning mid-argument. Throughout Romans 9–11, *Israel* has consistently meant ethnic, national Israel, and there is no textual signal that the meaning changes at this point. Nor does Paul suggest a salvation apart from Christ or apart from faith. Instead, he immediately grounds this hope in Scripture.

In verse 26, Paul quotes from Isaiah, pointing to the same Deliverer already proclaimed in the gospel:

- The Deliverer will come from Zion
- He will remove ungodliness from Jacob

Isaiah 59:20–21
20 "A Redeemer will come to Zion,
And to those who turn from transgression in Jacob," declares Yahweh.
21"As for Me, this is My covenant with them," says Yahweh:
"My Spirit which is upon you, and My words which I have put in your mouth shall not depart…"

This is not political restoration or cultural renewal. It is moral and spiritual rescue. Ungodliness is removed. Sin is dealt with.
Paul reinforces this in verse 27, quoting again:

27 "This is My covenant with them, When I take away their sins."

The future Paul describes is covenantal and redemptive. The same Christ who saves Gentiles by grace will apply that grace to Israel in fulfillment of God's promises.

What This Mystery Is—and Is Not

Notably, Paul does not stop to resolve every tension this raises. He does not yet explain how Israel can be both hardened and beloved, or how disobedience and mercy will finally converge.

He does not offer a timeline or mechanism.

That restraint is intentional.

This section is not meant to answer every question. It is meant to orient The Church—to read the present without arrogance and the future without despair.

Paul gives enough light to steady faith, not enough to satisfy speculation.

Why This Mystery Matters

Romans 11:25–27 functions as a hinge, not a conclusion. It keeps Gentile believers from pride, reassures Jewish believers of God's faithfulness, and prepares the way for what Paul will say next.

What follows will explain how Israel can be both disobedient and loved, how mercy triumphs without canceling justice, and how God's purposes have always been aimed at showing mercy to all (Romans 11:28–32).

Only then will Paul step back and worship.

14

Chapter 14

God's Mercy on a Timeline

Romans 11:28–32

Paul now draws together the strands he has been laying throughout Romans 9–11. He steps back far enough to help us see salvation history as a whole, and as he does, one truth comes into focus with steady clarity: God's plan is not driven by human deserving, but by divine mercy.

Paul is not merely informing the church; he is shaping its posture—guarding against pride, forgetfulness, and the subtle assumption that God's promises can be reinterpreted when they become uncomfortable. What follows is not speculation, but orientation.

The Text

28 From the standpoint of the gospel they are enemies for your sake, but from the standpoint of God's choice they are beloved for the sake of the fathers;

29 for the gifts and the calling of God are irrevocable.

30 For just as you once were disobedient to God, but now have been shown mercy because of their disobedience,

31 so these also now have been disobedient, that because of the mercy shown to you they also may now be shown mercy.

32 For God has shut up all in disobedience so that He may show mercy to all.

Two Standpoints, One Faithful God

In verse 28, Paul places two truths side by side that must not be separated.

From the standpoint of the gospel, Israel stands in opposition. Many have rejected the Messiah, and that rejection has become the occasion through which mercy has flowed outward to the nations.

From the standpoint of God's choice, however, Israel remains beloved. God's covenant commitments to the fathers have not expired, and they have not been quietly replaced or transferred elsewhere.

Paul is not contradicting himself. He is distinguishing perspective. One standpoint looks at Israel in relation to the present proclamation of the gospel. The other looks at Israel in relation to God's enduring covenant faithfulness. What is true in the unfolding mission of the gospel does not cancel what remains true in God's covenant promises.

Both are held together in the same faithful God—who judges unbelief honestly, extends mercy freely, and never abandons what He has sworn to uphold.

The Irrevocability of God's Promises

29 "For the gifts and the calling of God are irrevocable."

This sentence stabilizes the entire argument. God does not revoke what He has promised. His calling—His sovereign initiative and covenant purpose—is not fragile. His commitments are not provisional. Israel's present unbelief does not nullify God's prior word.

Paul is not minimizing Israel's need for repentance and faith. He has already made clear that salvation comes only through Christ. What he is denying is the idea that God abandons His promises when human obedience falters. God's faithfulness does not rise and fall with Israel's response.

A Pattern of Mercy Across History

Paul now steps back and traces the pattern of God's mercy as it unfolds across history. What he describes is not a sequence of accidents or divine reactions, but a purposeful movement shaped by God's sovereign design.

He reminds the reader that no group enters this story from a position of strength. Each stage exposes human disobedience and magnifies divine mercy.

Gentile Disobedience

Paul begins by reminding Gentile believers where they came from.

30a "For just as you once were disobedient to God…"

The Gentile past was not one of neutrality or simple ignorance. The nations suppressed truth, exchanged the knowledge of God for idols, and walked in open disobedience. Mercy did not arrive because the Gentiles were seeking God, but because God was seeking them. Their salvation began with divine grace, not human initiative.

Jewish Disobedience

Paul then turns to Israel with the same clarity.

30b "...but now have been shown mercy because of their disobedience,
31 so these also now have been disobedient..."

Israel's rejection of the Messiah is real and serious. Paul does not soften it. From the standpoint of the gospel, they stand opposed to the message they refuse. Yet even this disobedience unfolds within God's sovereign purpose. Israel's present unbelief has not surprised God, nor has it overturned His promises.

Mercy to the Gentiles—with Purpose

Gentile inclusion, Paul explains, is not an end point.

31 "...so that because of the mercy shown to you they also may now be shown mercy."

God's mercy toward the nations carries a forward-looking aim. As Gentiles receive grace through Israel's Messiah, Israel is meant to see what she has missed and to be drawn back, not through coercion, but through awakened longing.

Gentiles are not the climax of the story. They are recipients of mercy in the middle of it.

Mercy That Levels Everyone

Paul then gathers everything into a single, decisive statement.

32 "For God has shut up all in disobedience so that He may show mercy to all."

Throughout Romans 11, Paul has spoken in corporate terms—Israel and the Gentiles, not isolated individuals. When he says *all* here, he is gathering those same groups into a single verdict. Jews and Gentiles alike are enclosed under disobedience, so that mercy—not merit—receives the glory. No group enters God's favor by privilege, heritage, or moral advantage. All enter the same way—by mercy alone.

Paul's point is not that every person will be saved, but that no one is saved on different terms.

This does not teach universal salvation. Paul has already ruled that out repeatedly. Throughout Romans, salvation is consistently tied to repentance and faith in Christ (Romans 1:16–17; 3:22; 10:9–13). Judgment remains real, and unbelief remains accountable.

How Paul Reorients The Church

Paul's purpose here is not to blur or erase the story God has been writing across history, but to humble everyone who reads it by reorienting how God's mercy and judgment are understood over time.

- Israel cannot boast in heritage (Romans 11:28).
- Gentiles cannot boast in inclusion (Romans 11:30).
- The Church cannot boast in insight or timing (Romans 11:29).

Everyone stands on mercy.

God is not improvising. He is not reacting. He is not defeated by human unbelief. He is so sovereign that even disobedience becomes the dark backdrop against which His mercy shines more clearly.

15

Chapter 15

And So, Praise

Romans 11:33–36

Paul does not close Romans 11 with a final clarification, but with worship. After tracing God's mercy through Israel's stumbling, the Gentiles' inclusion, and the promise of restoration still to come, he reaches a point where the explanation has done its work—and praise is the only honest response.

He has just shown us God's mercy on a timeline. Now he shows us what mercy is meant to produce: wonder before God.

The Text

33 Oh, the depth of the riches and wisdom and knowledge of God! How unsearchable are His judgments and unfathomable His ways!
34 For who has known the mind of the Lord, or who became His counselor?
35 Or who has first given to Him that it might be repaid to him?
36 For from Him and through Him and to Him are all things. To Him be the glory forever. Amen.

Paul's movement is unmistakable. He has been teaching the church how to think clearly about God's mercy. But the goal was never information held at arm's length. Right doctrine is meant to bend the knee. Theology is not meant to terminate in understanding, but in worship.

Depths We Cannot Measure

Paul begins with three exclamations—three words that signal the limits of the creature and the greatness of the Creator.
33a Oh, the depth of the riches and wisdom and knowledge of God!

These are not abstract attributes. They are the living reality behind everything Paul has unfolded in God's saving work.
    The **riches of God** are the overflowing storehouse of His

mercy—kindness to the undeserving, patience with the disobedient, grace that does not originate in us and cannot be demanded by us (see also Romans 2:4; 9:23).

The **knowledge of God** is His perfect comprehension. Nothing surprises Him. Nothing is learned. Nothing comes into view too late.

The **wisdom of God** is His perfect application of that knowledge—always choosing the right ends and the right means to accomplish them.

Paul is not attempting to "solve" God. He is showing us why God cannot be solved. God's plan of redemption is not only powerful. It is wise. It is deeper than we can measure.

And because it is deeper than we can measure, Paul says:

33b How unsearchable are His judgments and unfathomable His ways!

"Unsearchable" means we cannot fully trace His decisions from the inside. "Unfathomable" means we cannot follow His paths the way we might track a human plan. God's footprints are not always visible to creatures who live inside time and see only part of the story.

That is not a defect in God's plan. It is a reminder that we are not God.

Three Questions That Silence Pride

Paul then does what Scripture often does at the edge of mystery: it humbles the reader—not to stop honest thinking, but to stop arrogant thinking.

34 For who has known the mind of the Lord, or who became His counselor?

Paul is echoing Scripture's insistence that God is never at a loss for wisdom, never short on perspective, never waiting for someone to supply insight He lacks. We only know what He reveals; we never stand over Him as evaluators.

Then he presses deeper.

35 Or who has first given to Him that it might be repaid to him?

This question is surgical. It strikes at the instinct beneath so much religion: the assumption that God can be put in our debt. That if we offer enough effort, sincerity, morality, devotion that now God owes us mercy as payment.

But Paul's whole argument has ruled that out. Mercy is not wages. Grace is not repayment. God is never the debtor.

This is where many people quietly feel the tension. Is it fair for guilty sinners to be forgiven freely? Is it just for mercy to be free?

Paul has already answered that earlier.

Romans 3:24–26

24 being justified as a gift by His grace through redemption, which is in Christ Jesus;

25 whom God displayed publicly as a propitiation in His blood through faith...

26 so that He would be just and the justifier of the one who has faith in Jesus.

God does not set aside justice in order to show mercy. He satisfies justice in order to show mercy. The cross is the place where justice is upheld and mercy is unleashed, so that no one can boast, and no one can accuse God of wrongdoing.

Taken together, these questions are meant to strip the reader of every posture that places God under evaluation, leaving us silent before His mercy rather than confident in our limited reasoning.

A Sentence That Puts Everything in Its Place

Paul ends with a sentence so comprehensive it becomes a lifelong re-calibration.

36 For from Him and through Him and to Him are all things. To Him be the glory forever. Amen.

Paul gives us three prepositions that place everything in its proper relation to God.

From Him: God is the source. Nothing ultimate begins with us.

Through Him: God is the sustainer and governor. Nothing

continues apart from His upholding power.

To Him: God is the goal. Nothing finds its true purpose until it terminates in His glory.

And because Paul is standing at the summit of everything he has said, he does not close with a caution or a command. He closes with the final purpose of all things—the glory of God.

36 To Him be the glory forever. Amen.

The Order of Grace

This book has not been written to solve God, but to right-size us before Him—clarifying where pride quietly intrudes and where a deeper, humbler trust can grow.

Across Romans 9–11, Paul has not offered a system to master, but a truth meant to humble the reader before God. He has shown us that God's choosing is not the result of our decision, but the reason any true decision toward Him is ever made. God does not choose because He sees something desirable in us. He chooses because He is merciful. And that mercy is free, purposeful, and unearned.

God's choosing is never arbitrary, but neither is it accountable to human standards of fairness. It flows from His own character, wisdom, and promises. He shows mercy where mercy magnifies His grace. He hardens where resistance has already taken root. And He does both without ever becoming unjust, unfaithful, or cruel.

This is the truth Paul has been guarding from distortion all along.

If we misunderstand how God chooses, we will either soften His sovereignty to protect our pride, or harden His character to protect our sense of control. Paul allows neither. He shows us a God who is absolutely sovereign and deeply good, a God whose mercy is wiser than our objections and whose judgments are purer than our instincts.

What Romans teaches us is not that God chooses *instead of* human responsibility, but that God chooses *before* it. Human belief is real. Human unbelief is accountable. But behind every act of saving faith stands a prior act of divine mercy.

This truth is not meant to produce fear in the believer, but rest.

Not anxiety, but humility.

Not speculation about others, but gratitude for grace.

We are not chosen because we believed well.

We believe because mercy found us first.

And once that truth settles, boasting dies. Comparison fades. Entitlement collapses. What remains is worship.

Paul ends here because faithful reasoning on this matter has reached its proper end. This is not the end of inquiry, but it *is* the end of pride. And that is exactly where understanding begins.

When the mind has been stretched to its limit and every illusion of control has been stripped away, the only fitting response is praise:

> For from Him and through Him and to Him are all things.
> To Him be the glory forever. Amen.

16

Conclusion

This book is not the final destination. It is the groundwork—so that what comes next can be offered to children with clarity, tenderness, and confidence in the kindness of God. If the Lord allows, the children's book that follows will carry these same truths in simpler form, for young hearts that need the same Savior.

About the Author

Joni Hyde writes as a fellow learner, not an expert standing at a distance. Her work has been shaped over many years by both discipline and disruption, and by a growing awareness that faith is not sustained by strength or insight, but by mercy.

Earlier seasons of her life were marked by structure, perseverance, and long-term commitment through work in physical fitness and training. Over time, however, loss, motherhood, and seasons of rebuilding redirected her attention toward deeper questions—questions not answered by effort or resolve, but by grace. Those seasons sharpened her desire to understand who God truly is, how His mercy works, and why faith rests more securely in what God does than in what we do.

Joni writes with particular care for parents and grandparents who want to pass on truth without fear or control, and who long for a theology sturdy enough to endure doubt, suffering, and ordinary life. Her aim is not to simplify God or resolve every mystery, but to present Him as He has revealed Himself—sovereign, good, patient, and faithful to His promises.

She is the mother of an adult daughter and a grandmother ("Mimi") to young grandchildren, whose lives have deepened her conviction that the most enduring faith is formed slowly, through truth spoken with gentleness and trust in God's kindness.

Joni lives in Little Rock, Arkansas, and continues to believe that grace changes lives—not all at once, but truly, deeply, and over time.